Primary science . . . taking the plunge

Aspects of the teacher's role in primary and middle school science teaching

Primary science . . .

taking the plunge

How to teach primary science more effectively

Edited by WYNNE HARLEN

Authors: Jos Elstgeest, Wynne Harlen, Sheila Jelly, Roger Osborne, David Symington

HEINEMANN EDUCATIONAL BOOKS

Heinemann Educational, a division of
Heinemann Educational Books Ltd
Halley Court, Jordan Hill, Oxford OX2 8EJ

OXFORD   LONDON   EDINBURGH
MADRID   ATHENS   BOLOGNA
MELBOURNE   SYDNEY   AUCKLAND
IBADAN   NAIROBI   GABORONE   HARARE
KINGSTON   PORTSMOUTH (NH)   SINGAPORE

First published 1985
Reprinted 1986, 1987, 1988 (twice), 1990 (twice)

ISBN 0 435 57350 0

Typeset by Fakenham Photosetting Ltd
Fakenham, Norfolk
Printed and bound in Great Britain by
Biddles Ltd, Guildford and King's Lynn

Preface

It is now widely recognized that science education involves children developing mental and manipulative skills and attitudes at the same time as forming ideas about the world around them. The emphasis on scientific process skills and attitudes places particular importance on the teacher's role, since it is not the choice of content of children's activities that determines the opportunities for these to develop as much as how the activities are carried out. It was to give some help in this matter of teaching methods that the present book was produced.

The chapters deal with features of the teacher's role that are known to cause concern to many teachers, particularly in primary schools: making a start, handling questions, encouraging children to make some kind of record of their work, helping them to raise questions, to observe, to plan investigations and taking into account children's own ideas. The authors have all worked for many years on the problems about which they write. They draw on their considerable experience to offer teachers advice which is soundly based on research into the teaching and learning of science.

Contents

1 Introduction: Why science? What science?

Wynne Harlen

This book is about the teacher's role in science activities. It attempts to fill some of the gaps in the help available to teachers, particularly those in primary and middle schools although most of its messages are relevant to teaching science at any stage of education. While there are literally hundreds of books available with ideas for classroom activities – that is, about what *children* might do – it is not easy to find help about what *teachers* might do. It is generally supposed that, in their activities, pupils use scientific process skills (see p. 4) and develop scientific concepts and attitudes, but whether or not this happens depends crucially on *the way* the activities are carried out as well as on what these activities are. Faced with this realization, some of the questions which come to teachers' minds are:

1 How do I encourage children to make a start?
2 How do I encourage them to observe more carefully?
3 What do I do if they ask questions I can't answer?
4 What do I do if they don't ask questions?
5 How do I get them to think about fair testing?
6 What should I do if they get the 'wrong' ideas?
7 How can I get them to write things down?

It is with these questions that this book is concerned. All the people who have contributed to it have been working in primary science education for many years and are writing about aspects of the teacher's role about which they have long been puzzling, researching and teaching.

The book does not pretend to be a comprehensive guide; there is nothing in it about making and storing equipment, for instance, nor about assessing children's development. Other books cover these topics (for example, Nuffield Junior Science, 1967, on resources and Harlen, 1983, on assessment). Yet with regard to finding answers to the questions above, things which are vital to good science teaching, it is curiously hard to come by substantial discussion and advice.

Advice at a practical level always derives from people's judgements about what children ought to be learning. These judgements, in turn, follow from a view of the nature of science and its role in education. Why are we teaching science at the pre-secondary stage and what kind of science is most appropriate? Answers to these are implicit throughout the various contributions, but it may be helpful to review them briefly here.

Why science?

Learning science helps children to develop ways of understanding the world around them. For this they have to build up concepts which help them link their experiences together; they must learn ways of gaining and organizing information and of applying and testing ideas. This contributes not only to children's ability to making better sense of things around them, but prepares them to deal more effectively with wider decision-making and problem-solving in their lives. Science is as basic a part of education as numeracy and literacy; it daily becomes more important as the complexity of technology increases and touches every part of our lives.

Learning science can bring a double benefit because science is both a method and a set of ideas; both a process and a product. The processes of science provide a way of finding out information, testing ideas and seeking explanations. The products of science are ideas which can be applied in helping to understand new experiences.

The word *can* is used advisedly here; it indicates that there is the potential to bring these benefits but no guarantee that they will be realized without taking the appropriate steps. In learning science the development of the process side and the product side must go hand in hand; they are totally interdependent. This has important implications for the kinds of activities children need to encounter in their education. But before pursuing these implications, there are still two further important points which underline the value of including science in *primary* education.

The first is that whether we teach children science or not, they will be developing ideas about the world around from their earliest years. If these ideas are based on casual observation, non-investigated events and the acceptance of hearsay, then they are likely to be non-scientific, 'everyday' ideas. There are plenty of such ideas around for children to pick up. My mother believed (and perhaps still does despite my efforts) that if the sun shines through the window on to the fire it puts the fire out, that cheese maggots (a common encounter in her youth when food was sold unwrapped) are made of cheese and develop spontaneously from it, that placing a lid on a pan of boiling water makes it boil at a lower temperature, that electricity travels more easily if the wires are not twisted. Similar myths still abound and no doubt influence children's attempts to make sense of their experience. As well as hearsay, left to themselves, children will also form some ideas which seem unscientific; for example, that to make something move requires a force but to stop it needs no force. All these ideas could easily be put to the test; children's science education should make children want to do just that and should provide them with the skills to do it. Then they not only have the chance to modify their ideas, but they learn to be sceptical about so-called 'truths' until these have been put to the test. Eventually they will realize that all ideas are working hypotheses which can never be proved right, but are useful as long as they fit the evidence of experience and experiment.

The importance of beginning this learning early in children's education is twofold. On the one hand the children begin to realize that useful ideas must fit the evidence; on the other hand they are less likely to form and to accept everyday ideas which can be shown to be in direct conflict with evidence and scientific concepts. There are research findings to show that the longer the non-scientific ideas have been held, the more difficult they are to change. Many children come to secondary science, not merely lacking the scientific ideas they need, but possessing alternative ideas which are a barrier to understanding their science lessons.

The second point about starting to learn science, and to learn scientifically, at the primary level is connected with attitudes to the subject. There is evidence that attitudes to science seem to be formed earlier than to most other subjects and children tend to have taken a definite position with regard to their liking of the subject by the age of 11 or 12. Given the remarks just made about the clash between the non-scientific ideas that many children bring to their secondary science lessons and the scientific ideas they are assumed to have, it is not surprising that many find science confusing and difficult. Such reactions undoubtedly affect their later performance in science. Although there is a lesson here for secondary science, it is clear that primary science can do much to avoid this crisis at the primary/secondary interface.

What science?

Science begins for children when they realize that they can find things out for themselves by their own actions: by sifting through a handful of soil, by blowing bubbles, by putting salt in water. The ideas they may have at the start of such actions may be changed as a result of what they do, what they see and how they interpret what happens. So the kind of science we are talking about concerns basic ideas which can emerge from simple investigations of objects and materials around. What ideas *do* emerge will depend not only on the events but on the way the children reason about them, on the way they process the information, that is, on their *process skills*. It is useful to divide these process skills into those concerned with information gathering and interpretation and those concerned with seeking explanations, hypothesizing and testing hypotheses.

PROCESS SKILLS

Information gathering	Generating and testing ideas
observing (and interpreting observations)	raising questions
	hypothesizing
interpreting information (pattern finding, inferring, predicting)	fair testing (experimenting)
	planning and carrying out investigations
communicating	

Fig. 1.1

Of course a rigid classification like this is not too helpful, since some process skills could be in both groups (observation and communication, for example). The value is in drawing attention to the importance of going beyond simply gathering information to trying to understand it and then testing out the new ideas that emerge. In this way the ideas the children develop are their own, ones which arise from their own thinking and not from someone else's view of the world.

To decide what experiences we want to give children in order to achieve our purposes we have to consider the children and not just the ideas and skills to be learned. 'Understanding the world around' means different things for a 5 year old, a 9 year old, a 13 year old, and so on, because their capacities for understanding are different and so are their worlds. The *ideas* of a young child will be those which fit his limited world. They will have to be modified and extended to fit his expanding experience and capacity. Likewise his *skills*, both intellectual and physical, will develop. For instance, in the matter of observation, a child will progress from making observations which are wide ranging and non-discriminating (but right for his present purpose) to making observations which are more focused, detailed and relevant to a particular problem (again right for his enlarged range of experience).

School science activities must take into account the way children learn at the primary level, that is, with thinking and doing closely related. Understanding depends on children working things out for themselves. This is *not* the same as saying that everything has to be discovered from scratch, but it does mean that children should be satisfied that the ideas they accept fit the evidence as far as they can tell. Some of these ideas may have been developed by the children themselves, offered by other children, by their teacher, or found in a book. In all cases the ideas must be related to evidence, subjected to critical examination and modified or reconstructed, if necessary, in the light of the evidence. This is where the process skills come in – to gather and interpret information, to devise and carry out fair tests and to communicate results.

So learning activities must allow process skills, attitudes (of critical reflection and healthy scepticism) and concepts to develop together. That is why the stress is laid on *how* children learn and not just *what* they learn. A particular activity could be carried out by some children just following instructions by rote or by other children thinking their way through from step to step. The difference is created by what the teacher does in preparation for, and during, the activity. Keeping children busy, physically active, is not the criterion for effective science teaching. Activity must be a vehicle for experience and thought, and thought is promoted by communication. The teacher's role in this process is crucial to children's learning and so we return to the reason for the existence of this book.

Science and other subjects

Many of the skills, attitudes and ideas that children learn from science activities are ones they could equally well learn, and certainly apply, in other areas of the curriculum. Observing, using patterns in information for predicting, inferring and drawing conclusions, come to mind as process skills that are relevant to a range of other areas of learning. There is a wide area of overlap between science and other subjects, just as there is among these other subjects themselves. It is generally acknowledged that the precise classification of an activity as 'science' or 'English' doesn't matter in the concept of topic work.

However, although many of the aims of science are the same as those in other areas of learning, it is important to realize that it is not so for *all*. There are some activities involving process skills, attitudes and concepts which are specifically scientific and are especially significant for that reason. The process skills are those relating to the testing of hypotheses (possible explanations) by experiment (fair testing). Although we can look at historical evidence, for instance, and suggest explanations, we cannot test these hypotheses by experiment, by re-running history. In science we not only can suggest, for example, that it is something to do with the light that make certain plants grow better in one place than another, but we can grow plants under controlled conditions and test whether the light makes a difference.

The concepts that are specifically scientific are those ideas that help the understanding of the order in the natural and physical world around; they are generalizations which emerge from the patterns that can be identified in natural materials and phenomena. They exist in the way the materials and things around behave and are open to everyone to observe. That a tree is a living thing is an idea that will occur to children when they have enough experience of trees and of other living things to see the connections. The idea that a tree is beautiful, awesome or symbolic, are conclusions of a quite different kind; not necessarily less important, but certainly different, from the ones which emerge from scientific enquiry. Thus science may be distinguished from other activities by the kinds of ideas children develop through using scientific methods of studying the things around them.

Most attitudes which we call scientific attitudes are common to the aims of other areas of the curriculum. Curiosity, perseverance, cooperation, open-mindedness, are important for all kinds of learning. But again we can distinguish some other attitudes which are more particularly 'scientific'; for instance, respect for the use of evidence in testing ideas and the critical reflection on experimental methods.

Thus, while it is true to say that some children may be 'learning science all the time' if their normal work is active and enquiry-based, it is likely that their learning in science will be limited if their activities do not involve them in:

1 Using the specifically scientific skills of investigating and experimenting to test ideas.
2 Generating and testing scientific ideas.
3 Reflecting critically on the way evidence has been gathered and used in testing ideas.

About the book

After the next chapter, about making a start – which logically comes first – the sequence of contributions has no particular significance. Readers may wish to dip into the chapters in numerical order or in the order that relates to their own priorities or concerns. To that end, a short outline is given at the beginning of each chapter and a detailed summary at the end, as well as a list of specific guidelines for practice. In fairness to the authors of the chapters, it should be noted that all the summaries and guidelines were written by the editor. The attempt to abbreviate inevitably distorts the message, so these concluding sections are no substitute for reading the whole chapters. The reader may find the outlines helpful in finding the chapters most interesting to them however, and as *aides-mémoire* later.

Outlines

Chapter 2

Objects around children provide invitations for enquiry – children observe and interact with objects – breaking down barriers – ways of overcoming the challenge to the teacher's confidence – encouraging children to learn from their environment – the importance of praise – accepting the child's observations and avoiding a search for the 'right' answer – giving children the time to observe and explore before searching for generalizations.

Chapter 3

Observation as a process influenced by preconceptions and expectations – various aspects of observation and how the teacher can improve children's skills – practical advice on how to extend observation skills.

Chapter 4

Types of questions needed to stimulate children's thoughts and actions – difference between productive and non-productive questions – types of productive questions – timing of questions – the problem of 'why' and 'how' questions.

Chapter 5

Helping children to raise questions – developing children's skills in asking productive questions – practical advice on developing this skill – establishing a suitable classroom climate – using surrounding objects to raise questions – turning 'difficult' questions from children into starting points for enquiry.

Chapter 6

The skills involved in planning – how planning helps children obtain information by enquiry – developing children's approach to problem-solving – helping children to test out ideas – ways children can participate in planning.

Chapter 7

Children's ideas about their world – how these ideas are or are not influenced by science teaching – action to change these ideas – appendix of actual lesson where teacher's and children's ideas conflict.

Chapter 8

Importance of children's communications – main channels of writing, talking, visual representation – discussion with whole class, groups, individuals – practical advice on use of children's notebooks – children's drawing, painting and modelling and how to use these skills in science.

2 Encounter, interaction, dialogue

Jos Elstgeest

Tiny Niels, beaming, bare and beautiful, crawled on the wet sand of the beach. He moved where the sea reaches out for the land, where the ocean barely touches the continent, where the exhausted waves drag themselves up the incline and withdraw or sink into the sand. Whenever this happened in slow and steady rhythm there appeared, all around Niels, tiny holes in the sand which bubbled and boiled with escaping air. These little marvels drew his attention, and with immense concentration he poked his finger in hole after hole, until a fresh wave wiped them all out and created new ones. Then Niels's game would start anew, until an unexpectedly powerful wave of the incoming tide knocked him over and, frightened, he gave up his play and cried.

Witnessing such a simple encounter between child and world, places all our well-learned treatises on child development and on the child's orientation in this world in the shadow. Here on this beach it happened. This was it. And we, adult know-alls, have nothing to add. The bubbling holes invited Niels: 'Come here, look at us, feel and poke.' And Niels did exactly that. He could not talk yet, not a word was exchanged, no question was formulated, but the boy himself was the question, a living query: 'What is this? What does it do? How does it feel?'

Question and answer converge here, flow together. The query of the child is the response to the challenge of the thing, of the bubbling holes. And the question coming from Niels as well as the answer he seeks and gets, passes through the same probing finger. A perfect interaction. Who dares interfere?

Countless such encounters occur in the lives of little people. Daily they meet with something new out of their world, and every time there is the invitation, the urge for interaction and dialogue: 'Look at me, feel me, handle me, try me, smell me, sniff me, lick me, taste me, hear me'.

It may be the clouds in the sky, or the birds in the under-growth; it may be a bumblebee on the clover, or a spider in a web, the pollen of a flower, or the ripples in a pond. It may be the softness of a fleece, the 'bang!!' in a drum, or the rainbow in a soapfilm. From all around comes the invitation; all around sounds the challenge. The question is there, the answer lies hidden, and the child has the key.

The problems of starting

Shall the key remain in the hands of the child? Who would not agree with me: 'But of course'. However, is this image, this interplay, this encounter between child and object, child and world clearly recognizable in the school? Is it obvious in your school, in your class with your own children? Wonder, asking, probing, and exploring form the key to science. And science is partaking, interaction, dialogue.

It is not surprising that many teachers find it difficult to intro-duce science education in their school in such a way that this interaction and dialogue are fully and effectively employed. It may even be difficult for children, particularly those who have become used to learning by rote. At one time I was asked to introduce the teachers of a school to this more open approach towards teaching children some science. I gladly accepted and walked into class three (mostly 9 year-olds) with a box full of mirrors. The best way to acquaint children with new materials is to bring them together and to let them 'mess about' a bit. With this intention I distributed the mirrors and did not say much. Mirrors appeal to children. Not one of them dared touch the mirror which was lying on their desk. In the middle of the class stood the regular teacher, a kind but firm person with a 'don't-you-dare' smile on her face. The kids just sat there, arms folded.

When I tried to encourage them to do something with their mirrors, they shyly and slyly took a peep, giggled and quickly put the mirror down again. It was no use. The atmosphere in the classroom, the regimental arrangement of the desks and, not least, the dominant presence of their teacher were too great a barrier. No encounter, no interaction, no dialogue was possible. There was no room for interplay, so after a few minutes I took them out of the classroom and outdoors.

Their first discovery was that holding the mirror over your

eyes turns the world, and everything in it, upside-down. They chased each other's topsy-turvy image trying to touch it.

Soon we started a game. 'Who can walk along the snaky line drawn on the ground without missing a curve once?' The trick was that they had to look in the mirror held over their eyes. This was not easy. They looked up into their mirrors and tried to find their way in this inverted world. They could not get enough of it and made it increasingly more difficult for each other by drawing slinky lines with sharp corners and hairpin bends, while keen eyed sentries kept watch so that nobody would stealthily look down.

They abandoned this exercise when they discovered that they could reflect sunlight wherever they wanted with their mirror. Now their teacher was in for a rough time as she became the children's first target. She bore it bravely, be it with obviously mixed feelings. I took the burden off her by chasing the light spots which the children reflected onto the blind wall at the back of the school. Soon I was joined by other children and it developed into a game: whoever could 'catch' somebody's light spot knocked him out, and they were to change places. The children holding the mirrors faced the problem of figuring out which of the reflections dancing on the wall was their own, so they could divert it when somebody made a dash for it. When the bell rang, and we returned to the classroom, I was pleased to notice three children under a hedge patiently following a giant ant which pulled a big cockroach by a leg towards its lair. The children wanted to know where the ant would drag the roach and whether he would eat it.

This incident illustrates the happy side of versatile childhood. The barriers are easily taken down, the bonds readily broken, and dialogue is established once more. However on the part of the teacher, too, some impediments must be removed. Vague fears plague the teacher often. 'Will I not lose authority?' 'What do I do with the deluge of children's questions?' 'Will the whims of the children take over once discipline is gone?' This initial lack of confidence is uncomfortable but real, so, before we take the plunge, let us consider a few principles and guidelines.

Briefly, what do we want to achieve in our science lessons? We want to give the children the opportunity to develop their own powers of reasoning; to increase their ability to solve problems in a scientific way in pace with their intellectual development, and so to allow them to meet new events and experiences and inter-act with these on their own terms. The teacher's task is then to work closely with the children, to enrich their environment by providing stimulating materials, to put the right question at the right time and to encourage the children to pursue their interests.

'Doing science' with the smallest children has a special flavour. One cannot talk about formal lessons here, of course, but one can definitely and fruitfully organize 'activity periods' during which the 'encounter, interaction and dialogue' are encouraged. The main task of the teacher here is to provide ample materials for the children to work with. Any odds and ends are useful and they may be just everyday things, for common oddities are for children often less common than we realize.

It is not necessary during activity periods that all of the children do the same thing at the same time. A few containers of different shape and size, bits of hose pipe, a few funnels, perhaps a larger tub or pail, squeeze bottles, tins with and without holes and a few small cups are enough to keep six to ten children happily busy with water activities. They fill and refill containers, matching volumes and counting; they explore leakages, aim squirts, invent syphons, communicate vessels, and do a thousand and one other activities that the teacher would never think of but children do. Paints or colours may be in short supply and serve only four or five children at a time, but others can work with wet sand making shapes, or with dry sand sieving and sorting or weighing. A few available tools may be given to one or two constructing enthusiasts, while the remaining children build with blocks and boxes. As long as there are sufficient materials it is never difficult to keep a class occupied, but it does mean breaking the class up into working groups and reorganizing the room so that the working groups do not interfere with each other.

The inexperienced teacher might be apprehensive: 'But I cannot keep an eye on all of them. They will get up to all sorts of naughty things.' Will they? When children have sufficient materials and are free to work with them to make their own genuine explorations and discoveries, then they have no more reason for being 'naughty'. Noise there will be, certainly, for children are noisy when they become excited, and they talk a lot. But this is part of the intention. Through talking they learn to use language. Besides, talking helps you understand better what it is you are doing. It also strengthens a spirit of cooperation. And children who are learning to work cooperatively are sensitive and sensible enough to learn how they can and should avoid disturbing others unduly. This may be momentarily forgotten in the heat of some argument, or at the peak of some hilarious event, but it is never difficult to remind the children. An active class can be a very happy one and most rewarding to the children as well as to the teacher. There need be no fear of chaos as long as there is understanding between the teacher and children.

A positive aspect of children working in groups is that they can concentrate on what they are doing and on each other. They may be completely unaware of their teacher for quite long periods, leaving the teacher free to give attention to single groups of children, to individuals who need help or who want to talk about their work, or to those who want to show what they have made or discovered.

From time to time the whole class may be engaged in doing the same project. An excursion to the local park to collect interesting things, for instance, or playing games that involve a larger group. Groups should get together to tell each other about what they have been doing and what they have found. Working in groups does not mean that the class as a whole loses its identity. Nor does the teacher cease to take a central part in providing for the children's learning. The presence of the teacher is very important indeed, for thoughtful organization, friendly persuasion, provision and storage of materials, helpful advice and, sometimes, just plain assistance in need is something that only a good teacher can provide.

As children grow in age and intelligence, their activities become less random, their interests more specific, and their approach to problem solving more sophisticated. Naturally, the teacher must adapt too. In the middle and upper classes of the primary school, and beyond, the teacher's role becomes more and more that of a leader towards specific goals that the children set for themselves, or that they accept being set for them. This requires special skills and attitudes on the part of the teacher. These skills will mainly pertain to the teacher's own experience of doing science, while the attitudes should be based on the statement that 'the teacher should encourage the children to continue experimenting and exploring (= learning) in the direction of their interests.'

Ways of encouraging children to learn from the things around them

Appreciation, not admonition

Sincere appreciation has a more positive effect on children's behaviour than the threat of punishment. This appreciation should be directed not so much to the product, but to the effort of the child. In their science activities the children explore some aspect of their environment. They try to learn from it by investigating possibilities and solving broad or specific problems. Depending on circumstances like age, ability, past experience and available materials, the products of the children's scientific efforts will vary in quality, but may all look clumsy in comparison with the achievements of the great scientists of the past. So do not make this comparison. The children are looking for and finding answers to their problems by their own efforts, and it is not the answers, but the efforts of the working children that deserve our encouragement and appreciation. This is what the teacher must learn to understand, for this is where the struggle begins for the 'right' answer.

Children's ideas and the 'right' ideas

Somewhere in the conscience of every teacher lies a sense of duty concerning 'the truth', and rightly so. However, teachers do tend to take a rather absolute and dogmatic view where 'the truth' is concerned. We are inclined to think that we ought to present the children with the truth and that is where the basic mistake is made. Scientific activity, and also that of the children, is directed towards detecting the truth as it reveals itself in the reality of the things we study. Therefore, we must begin to look for a new kind of 'right' answer. We must begin to look for a right answer which the children can give with confidence, which depends on their own observations: a right answer which originates from their experiences. This right answer may fall short of 'the truth'. In other words, we are concerned with, and interested in, what the searching child finds out, what he observes, what he has to think and to say about his experiences. The professional scientist, too, would produce his experience and his evidence in order to corroborate what he regards and expresses as true fact. Thus we should not ask a child what somebody else thinks, but what he himself thinks is true.

The reason for this new kind of 'right' answer is that we are anxious to help the child to think clearly and independently. If we, as teachers, are of a different opinion concerning what is true – as with good reason we often are – then a blunt 'wrong!' would still be out of place. First of all, we might well be wrong ourselves. Secondly, 'right' and 'wrong' do not depend on our authority, but on the authority of the real facts which may have been incompletely explored by the child. Further observation may well correct the child's original statement of fact, and that is what we mean by 'encouraging the child to continue experimenting in the direction of his own interest'.

For instance, when I worked with antlions* and children, I found that children at first were convinced that antlions eat dust. Their fresh experience shows them that an antlion sits at the bottom of a dusty pit for a long time. That the creature patiently waits for some bait, like an ant, to stray into the pit so he can catch and eat it, is not yet part of their experience. What is part of their daily experience, however, is that one should eat in order to stay alive. So, if the antlion lives, he must eat the only thing that seems to be available to him: dust. What happens if we now say to the children, 'No, that is wrong'? Naturally, the idea of dry dust being food is absurd to us, but will the children be any happier with our statement? This would only imply that they were wrong in the eyes of the teacher for, at this stage, they have no way of understanding any better. The teacher's authoritative statement has in no way enriched the children's experience of the truth. Further experience, however, is bound to make the children change their mind about what antlions eat. So continue to let the children observe the antlions in action until they have enough evidence to make them change their minds.

Letting the children persist in this obviously faulty opinion was too much for one conscientious teacher. He persuaded the children to go and feed ants to the antlions 'so you can see what they really eat'. They did this and the teacher contentedly thought: 'that settles the mistake'. Later, when the teacher looked through the children's notebooks, he found to his amazement that, 'Antlions eat dust. But if they get an ant, they eat that too'. The last bit was a concession to their teacher, for they were just convinced that ants are no more than a welcome supplement to the antlion's dusty diet.

Experience before generalization

Children naturally seek the approval of the adult in whose care

* Throughout the tropics, and in many temperate lands except in the British Isles, lives an insect larva which digs neat little round pits in loose soil or sand. At the bottom of the pit lurks the larva, its saw-edged pincers at the ready to receive, pierce and consume any venturous insect which happens to stray over the edge and consequently slither to the bottom. Since this frightful fate most often befalls busy ants, the predator is called an antlion. However, the larva is completely harmless to children; it is clean and hardy, can be handled freely, and needs only some loose soil to find its natural surroundings. It is therefore a perfect little animal for study in the classroom and outside.

they have been placed, and this approval is a very strong form of encouragement. Let us consider the following case. Children observe insects through magnifying glasses and become involved in their intricate structure. They have no experience of the respiratory systems of insects and naturally assume that they breathe through their mouth. They do notice, however, that a grasshopper's abdomen expands and contracts rhythmically. They also notice tiny dot-like marks along the length of the insect's abdomen. To the children these two phenomena are not in the least related. Yet they say, 'Look, my insect is breathing'.

Now if at this stage the teacher comes along and asks, 'How does your insect breathe?', the only possible answer the children can give is, 'through its mouth'. They are being put in a position of having to answer wrongly. The idea of insects breathing through holes in their abdomens is simply too far beyond the children's experience to be comprehensible. The children's answers were not really wrong; the teacher was wrong in asking this question. What the teacher could have asked is, 'What is your grasshopper doing?' or, 'Have you seen anything new or unusual?' To this type of question the children can give a right answer, truthfully and confidently, and uninhibited by fear of disapproval.

When children study insect structure, they are bound to find differences with more familiar structures. They cannot fail to find many details odd. They become aware of the unique charac-ter of another structure and questions on function may arise, some answers to which may be found. The study of insect structure, among other studies, helps the children to become conscious that there are many different kinds of structure among living things. They are adding to their store of experiences, which is an essential prerequisite to their later ability to generalize, a process we cannot hasten unduly. Therefore, we are not interested in what the syllabus or the book has to say on insect structure. We are interested in what the child himself has thought about insect structure. We must attempt to work with the children in such a way that they freely give us their own right answers: the observations and thoughts about their own experi-ences.

This requires much tact and understanding, and one of the first tasks of the teacher is to assure the children that it is not only the teacher who decides what is important to study and what is not, but that they decide it together.

When a teacher in Tanzania took her class out to observe the masses of dragonflies which persistently followed them wherever they walked through the grassy fields of Bukima, along Lake Victoria, they started out with the question, 'Why do those dragonflies follow us?' The children were intrigued by the behaviour of the insects, but it soon turned out that finding the answer was very difficult. Soon, the majority of children were busy with something else. Dungbeetles, shoving dungballs along the ground had attracted their attention. Noticing this, the teacher no longer insisted on pursuing the riddle of the dragonflies. Instead she diverted her attention to what the children were actually doing and joined them in their research. This led to a two-week study of dungbeetles and their behaviour, their food and their skill in rolling balls, their life history which was hidden in specially made balls but uncovered by the children, their homes and hiding places. It was a busy, involved and hardworking class, where teacher and children made scores of exciting discoveries.

A minority of these children, however, persisted in pursuing the antics of the dragonflies and, of course, the teacher let them, and worked with them too. The children beat the dragonflies down, so they could observe them more closely. They thus distinguished and sorted seven different kinds of dragonflies. In the process of beating them down they noticed that some dragonflies had their abdomen sliced off, yet they did not die and kept trying to fly away. By putting a piece of straw into the remaining segment the children made the wounded insects regain their balance and away they flew to the loud cheers of the children. Via many diversions this group came very close to an answer to their original question, when they saw dragonflies actually catching other small insects which had been disturbed by the movement of feet in the grass. And this answer: 'They follow us because we chase the lakeflies which they eat,' was based on the authority of their experience and not on the authority of an alien text. The teacher encouraged her children in the direction of their interest. More, she encouraged the encounter and took part in the interaction and dialogue between children and insects.

Negative encouragement

One more example illustrates how one can effectively discourage children. An inexperienced teacher handed out glasses of water and corks to a class four (mainly 10 year-olds). Corks behave in their own way when they float in glasses of water. If the glass is only partly filled, they go to the side, but if the glass is full and has a bulging meniscus, the cork floats in the centre. The teacher had set his mind on making the children discover this.

For a while Anna and her partner Rose watched the cork bob on the surface of the water. They found nothing really exciting about this and had quickly seen it. Soon they began to experiment with other objects. Their pencil, stuck into the water to hold the cork down, appeared to be bent. Rose's finger seemed huge when seen through the side of the glass. Then they tried the inkwell, one of those old-fashioned ones made of porcelain with a hole in the top. Funny. It sank slowly at first, as it filled with water, and then all of a sudden sank to the bottom. By the time the teacher on his rounds came to talk to the pair, they had completely forgotten about the cork bobbing on the surface.

'What do corks do on the water?' began the teacher. Anna and Rose looked at each other in obvious bewilderment. 'Float' murmured Anna. 'And', inquired the teacher, 'why do you suppose they float?' Some question! It took an elderly Archimedes to figure that one out, so what can you expect from class four girls? After a painful pause Rose and Anna had to admit that they did not know. The teacher then suggested that they try more experiments to find out. But what experiments to find out exactly what? And, as the teacher left them to go and upset other children, the two girls, dutifully but with no interest, started bobbing the cork on the surface of the water once more.

What did the teacher learn about the two girls and their work? He only found out that they did not know why corks float. And what did Rose and Anna learn? They learned that they had made a 'mistake'. They had displeased the teacher because they did not give him his 'right answer'. The discoveries they did make no longer seemed important to them, for the teacher wanted to know something else of which they had no idea.

By not listening to them the teacher missed an important chance to encourage his girls. Perhaps he missed a chance to experience something new himself. He missed an opportunity to make the girls learn more. They were interested in a really curious phenomenon, the funny way an inkwell sinks. As it happened he blocked their learning at the moment altogether, but what would have happened if the teacher had watched and listened for a while to the two girls before he decided to interfere?

He would have noticed what they were actually doing. He could have started with, 'What is happening here?' and the girls would have shown him the curious behaviour of the inkwell sinking in the water. 'You see, it goes slowly at first, and then it sinks fast. Look!' might have been their commentary. The teacher seeing their problem might then have asked: 'Have you watched how the water moves over the top of the inkwell?' and the girls would have eagerly made this part of their observation in their next experiment. The teacher could have left with the casual suggestion, 'I wonder if you could make the inkwell float.'

Partnership in learning

If the teacher really wants to encourage the children, then he must first assure them that he is interested in what they are actually doing. Once the children are sure that their teacher is genuinely interested in their work, they will gain the confidence which is essential to talk freely and truthfully about it. They will be interested in what the teacher has to contribute to the conversation and to further investigation. They will be ready to assimilate his explanations, for the teacher has now become part of, and partner in, the encounter, the interaction and the dialogue.

Summary of main points

This chapter has been all about starting – that difficult time when something new and unfamiliar has to be attempted. Such occasions can make us feel uncomfortable. Teachers and children can reject strange new experiences because these don't conform with what is usual, what is expected. Making a start therefore needs careful planning as well as determination.

Ideas have been suggested for making a start with very young children and with older children, noting the appropriate differences in the children's activities and in the teacher's role. Once begun, learning by encounter with materials will prosper if the conditions are right, but wither under discouragement even if this is unintentional. Teachers have to be careful not to discourage, but take positive steps to encourage children's activity and thinking. Some important ways of encouraging children are through:

1 Appreciating children's efforts whatever their results may be.
2 Avoiding the suggestion that the only worthwhile result is the 'right answer' in terms of correct facts and conclusions.
3 Accepting what the children find from their investigation as the 'right answer', providing they have used their evidence and their reasoning.

4 Allowing children to make sense of their observations for themselves without imposing explanations which are outside their experience and comprehension.

From the discussion the following guidelines emerge:

Guidelines for starting

1 Make sure that plenty of materials are available (most that serve this purpose are not expensive).
2 Make sure the materials interest the children (listen to them and watch them to find what interests them).
3 Provide a situation in which children feel free to make their start by playing.
4 Remove any structure in the classroom which appears to inhibit this play.
5 Create a structure which facilitates play – a challenge, a task, preferably one which children can tackle in a group cooperatively.
6 Allow and encourage children to talk about what they are doing, to you and to each other.

Guidelines for encouraging the encounter once it has started

1 Show appreciation of the children's efforts to solve their problem or carry out a task, whatever the outcome.
2 Accept an answer or result that is consistent with the observations the children have made and the evidence that is available to them.
3 Expect children to offer their own ideas about what they have found, not to know and repeat some supposed 'right' ideas.
4 Show that you respect ideas that fit the evidence; ask for evidence and accept whatever ideas fit it.
5 Focus your questioning and the children's attention on widening the range of observations rather than on reaching premature conclusions.
6 Listen to the children's answers and ideas and use them as a starting point for further reasoning and enquiry.

3 Helping children to observe

Wynne Harlen and David Symington

Introduction

It would be widely agreed that observation is a skill of central importance in primary science education. Observation ranks high in the aims and objectives of all primary science programmes, in teachers' goals and in what they emphasize in activities (see Chapter 6, pages 66, 67). So we shall not spend time making the case for the importance of observation. What we are more concerned about in this chapter is to show that there is a case for helping children to observe more effectively and to focus on the teacher's role in improving children's observation skills.

We began with some points about the nature of observation and various aspects of the skill, then give some evidence from research to show that there is room for improvement, followed by a short summary of the roles of observation in children's learning. In the final section, suggestions are made about teaching strategies and procedures which help children to observe more effectively.

About observation

Observation is the process through which we come to take notice, to become conscious, of things and happenings. It can involve the use of any of the senses alone or in combination. But taking in information by observation is not like soaking up water into a sponge. The senses do not absorb everything that is there; they function selectively and the selection is influenced by existing ideas and expectations. Our existing concepts and knowledge affect what we see or hear or feel. For instance, two people observing the same formation of clouds in the sky may observe quite different things about them. One, who knows little about clouds except that they block out the sun and bring rain, may see only their extent across the sky and their darkness. Another, who knows the significance of different features of clouds, may be able to report on their probable height, depth, direction of movement, changing formation and be able to predict further changes from these observations. The well-known story of the vicar and the entomologist walking in the churchyard is another example. The sound of the choir singing in the church mingled with the whistling of the crickets and other early evening noises of the countryside. The vicar expressed his appreciation of the lovely sound they were hearing. The entomologist agreed: '. . . and it's wonderful to think that it comes from their back legs'. Though the physical sounds were available to both, what each heard was different.

In the classroom this means that not everyone observes the same things, even though they may be there for all to notice. Take the example of the teacher who was hoping to show a group of children that a candle under a jar would burn for longer the larger the jar. He had three jars of different size and explained to the boys how to put them over three burning candles all at the same time. It worked well. So when the teacher asked them what differences they saw between the jars he was disappointed in their reply. 'Nothing. It was same for all of them. All the candles went out.' None of the boys had observed what the teacher hoped they would notice – the difference in time of burning in each jar, a difference quite large enough to be noticed by someone looking for it. The teacher might easily have assumed that because the difference was observable it therefore had been observed. We shall return later to discuss how a teacher might deal with situations of this kind.

Another example of how our knowledge and concepts influence what is observed is provided by a teacher travelling with school children in the Netherlands. The teacher was struck by the sight of the water level in the canals being several metres above the surrounding pastures. But this was not mentioned by any of the children who later described the canals, boats, cows and pastures they had seen. It seems likely that the children did not share the teacher's expectations that the level of water in waterways is usually below that of the surrounding countryside, and therefore they just did not take in this information.

What this means is not that we are totally blinkered by what we already know and never see beyond it, but it does suggest that developing the ability to observe and building up ideas go hand in hand (see also Chapter 1). Developing the skills of observing enables children to seek consciously for information which will extend their ideas. The teacher's role in this development is to provide opportunities for using the different aspects of observation, often through discussion or through providing problems whose solutions require a wide range of observations to be made and brought together. While this is happening, not only will the children be extending their ideas and understanding of the particular things they observe, but they will also be developing skills which can be applied to other problems and situations. So the extension of ideas and understanding is accompanied by a development of the skill of observation and depends to some extent upon it.

Aspects of the skill of observing

We shall be more explicit about the different aspects of observation and how they help the formation of ideas.

Observing details

A favourite activity given by one teacher of 11 year olds at the start of their school year is to give them each a lighted candle and a blank sheet of paper. The children are asked to write down their observations of the candle flame. Their descriptions vary enormously in detail. Many children are like the one who stopped after writing: 'It is yellow and pointed at the top. It flickers.' By contrast take the account of another: 'The flame is blue at the bottom, turns yellow higher up and tapers to a darker, feathery tip. Inside the whole there is a smaller, darker flame of the same shape. The shape is always changing as the flame flickers.' The teacher finds that discussing these descriptions leads the children back to make more observations, which sometimes settles disputed points but sometimes leads to everyone revising and refining their account. She is not so much (in fact hardly at all) interested in what they learn about the flame, but in what they learn about how much they can find out by looking. Then, when they are looking at other things, which *are* ones they want to find out about, she asks them the same kinds of questions as helped them refine their observations of the candle – about the shape, size, colour of each feature, whether it changes or is the same all the time and, if it changes, in what ways and what else changes at the same time, and so on. So, whether it is a caterpillar or a crystal growing in a solution, the children learn to get information *from the object* by consciously looking in detail at its features.

The value of observing details as opposed to only more global features is that it often helps in making sense of other observations. One child may look at a caterpillar and see that it has seven pairs of legs spread out along its body. Another child may notice the differences between the shape and movement of the three pairs of walking legs and the four pairs of cushion feet. The second child is obviously in a better position to relate the caterpillar's legs to those of the butterfly after metamorphosis and to the generalization that insects have three pairs of legs.

Observing similarities and differences

Children's senses are acute and they are well able to detect small points of difference between two fairly similar objects. They enjoy the quiz book game of 'spotting the mistakes' in two almost similar pictures. But what makes this difficult in a quiz context is not the sensitivity of vision required, it is that the mistakes are totally random. There is no pattern in what one is looking for and one observation does not give a clue to another. Observation in the context of science activities is not like this. Here there is a purpose to the observation of differences, which is often to detect a set of conditions or properties which helps to explain something or solve a problem. The listing of all possible differences confuses the issue and may mean that a useful pattern is more difficult to pick out. For instance, when some children were finding out how to distinguish between eggs which were solid inside and those which were still liquid inside, they first made various observations of differences between eggs known to be cooked and others which were not cooked. They listed differences in movement of the eggs (rolling and spinning), in the sounds they made when tapped, in what happened when the eggs were put in tap water and in salty water, and so on. It would not have helped them for this investigation to have added that the shells were slightly different textures and that one had a blue label and one a red one. Thus children have to learn to distinguish relevant from non-relevant differences in terms of the problem in hand or the reasons for their observation.

The observation of similarities is perhaps more important than that of differences, yet is not so often given attention. To see that, despite their many differences, two objects in Figure 3.1 have something in common, is to recognize the broader ideas –

Fig. 3.1 *Despite the differences, these have enough in common for us to identify them both as objects for sitting on.*

the concepts and generalizations – which link together things which differ in various respects. Such broad ideas are essential to human understanding; without them we would be at a loss to cope with the variety of objects and events which surround us. The formation of these concepts depends upon the recognition of similarities of certain kinds between things and this is a skill needed in situations where everything seems to be different. Essential to it is to be able to see that different groupings can be produced by giving attention to different features. So, for example, the cat, dog and canary fall in the same group if we focus on the observation that these are often found in people's homes, or on the possession of a tail, but fall in different groups if we consider other features of their anatomy or their food. Again, the three pendulums in Figure 3.2 are alike in one way (a) or in another way (b) or in yet another way (c).

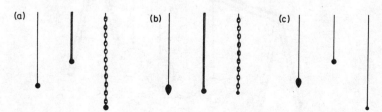

Fig. 3.2

Part of observing more effectively is to apply knowledge that some similarities and differences are more important than others. Children will eventually find this out by exploring with the pendulums. This information then becomes part of the children's background knowledge of pendulums which will help them 'filter out' differences of no consequence, just as in the earlier example of the eggs where the colour of the labels can be regarded as a non-relevant difference.

Observing events and sequence

Often it is the relationships between one observation and another, rather than any one individually that helps in the understanding of events. For example, a child might observe that a cold can of drink taken out of the fridge has moisture on it. The understanding of why this is so will be helped by making observations in a sequence. Was there moisture on the can when it was in the fridge? When does it appear? What happens if the can is left out of the fridge for a long time? Does it appear if an empty can is used? Similarly, careful observation of the process of coloured ink being soaked up by blotting paper helps a child to grasp how the different constituent colours can be separated, so chromatography can become a phenomenon within his understanding, rather than something that happens like magic.

Detecting patterns in observations

The association of one observation with another has already been mentioned in relation to similarities and differences and sequences. Detecting patterns in observations takes this a step further; it often requires looking to and fro between the observations and ideas about possible patterns. For example in the

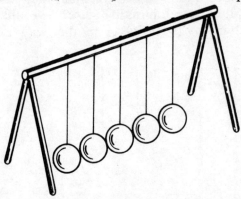

Fig. 3.3

'Newton's cradle' toy (Figure 3.3), if one ball is drawn aside and let go, another ball swings away at the opposite end. If two balls are taken together, two swing away. This suggests a pattern, but to verify it, other observations would have to be made. Here the hypothesized pattern is focusing further observation. Similarly, patterns can be established in observations of weather conditions at the simplest level of associating clouds with rain to the more complex patterns used in weather forecasting. The use of patterns in observations for making predictions and for suggesting explanations shows very clearly how this process skill helps in the development of ideas and generalizations which represent our understanding of phenomena in the world around us.

How well do children observe?

There is no straight answer to this question, but some careful assessment of children's performance on various aspects of observation has produced findings which raise serious questions about present practice.

The APU* surveys carried out in England, Wales and Northern Ireland between 1980 and 1984 included practical tests in which various observation tasks were given to children aged 10 to 11 years. The results from the first two surveys can be summarized as follows (DES 1983).

Observing details

- A very large majority of children's observations concerned gross features rather than more detailed ones.
- Performance in questions where observation was directed to certain details showed that children were able to see details when asked to give attention to them.

Observing similarities and differences

- Children were more fluent in noticing differences than similarities.
- In general they confined their observations to points relevant to the task in hand.
- Children were well able to use senses other than sight to help in describing or identifying objects.

* Assessment of Performance Unit.

- In grouping objects on the basis of similarities and differences, mistakes were often the result of noticing only gross features and neglecting details.
- Success in grouping objects was at a higher level than explaining the reasons for objects fitting into one group or another.

Observing events and sequence

- Children were more successful in selecting a sequence from possible alternatives than in reporting a sequence in their own words after being shown a sequence of events.
- After watching an event take place, their reports indicated that they had only 'seen' the result, not the process of arriving at it.

Detecting patterns in observations

- Performance was acceptable in making a prediction based on observations of a series of events, though not all children who made a satisfactory prediction could describe the observations they used in arriving at it.
- Many children did not seem to have made the observations necessary to detect a pattern in events shown to them, and few (about one in fifteen) succeeded in expressing related observations in terms of a pattern.

The need for improvement

Although these results were obtained in three countries of the UK, they are likely to be typical of children's performance in many other countries. In summary they add up to a picture of children under-using their senses. The arguments for changing this situation are based on the evidence, and the belief, that children's ability in the various aspects of observation can be improved and that this would benefit their science education. These benefits can be summarized as follows:

Using observation to help concept development

Much has been said about this already and perhaps all that need be added is to stress that observations have to be brought together and connected with each other. The benefit will not follow if they are left as isolated observations. Take, for example, the children whose teacher helped them observe the condensation of water vapour from a boiling kettle on to a cold plate. In discussing this they were quickly able to relate this observation to the fogging of the windows in the kitchen when vegetables are being boiled and to the misting of the mirror in the bathroom when a bath is being run. From these observations they could pick out what was similar about the conditions in which water vapour was condensed and this helped them understand the process of condensation.

Using observation to extend knowledge of the natural, physical and technological world

The simple observation that a pencil appears to be thickened when placed in a jar of water shows that water can act in the same way as a magnifying glass. Detailed observation of the natural world cannot fail to bring awareness of the rich diversity of plants and animals. For example, when groups of pupils were given small patches of a field to examine the teacher found the same reaction from all the groups. They were amazed at the number of different plants there were in such a small area.

Using observation to stimulate scientific investigation

Clearly observation is an essential part of a scientific enquiry. It comes in at all stages. It may be the stimulus to enquiry, as when some children studying bones from various animals noticed that some were different colours. 'Do different coloured bones come from different animals?' was the start of an investigation.

Using observation to help draw conclusions from investigations

Although many other process skills, discussed in other chapters, are involved in scientific investigation, observation has a particularly important part to play since the *quality* of observations made is a significant factor determining whether meaningful conclusions can be drawn. But the link between what is found and the original problem is often not made – comparisons or other observations are recorded, but not taken further. Children observing that a spiral of thin card rotates when suspended over a candle flame often have to be helped to connect this with their original investigation of what happens to air when it is heated. Does the movement of the spiral mean that the air is moving upwards? Why not downwards? To answer this means looking again not just at whether the spiral turns, but in which direction and to find out if this is consistent with air moving upwards through it. The attempt to use evidence in this way sends children back to make more observations and so refines this skill at the same time as making use of it.

Helping children to observe

Activities designed specifically to give children practice in observing, such as the observation of a candle flame (page 23), should be rare events. If used too frequently they defeat their own end, since they quickly become boring and provoke an unthinking routine reaction. For the most part, observation is best developed in the activities in which it is used. It serves various purposes, so what a teacher might do to encourage effective observation will depend upon the role of observation in the activity.

Contributing to concept development

The two most important steps the teacher can do to promote observation for this purpose are to provide opportunities for observation and for discussion of observations.

Opportunity means that there is access to appropriate materials and events with the time to make observations in detail and in depth and, if necessary, to repeat and refine them. The materials for observation should be selected so that observations can be made which are relevant to the concepts or generalizations the teacher has in mind. This does not mean highly structured 'set pieces', but that some thought is given to the materials. For example, children may understand a great deal more about the development of fruits and seeds if they are able to observe fruits at different stages of maturity than if they are given only one fruit to examine. They might be asked to try to put the fruits in a sequence of maturity and to say what features led them to choose that sequence. Through this they find out at first hand about the changes which accompany development of seeds.

Time is an important dimension in providing opportunity to observe. Many children seem to observe only superficially and to lose interest within minutes. But these same children often return to the objects after the chance to think and particularly after discussion. For example, the boys who at first saw no difference between the candles being under the different sized jam jars were fascinated by their 'discovery' when their teacher asked them to look particularly at whether the candles all went out at the same time when the experiment was repeated. Then they wanted then to do it again and again and each time they became more sure of what they saw.

Discussion is a process relevant to all purposes of observation. Its qualities and management are discussed in Chapter 8, since these are generally applicable to pursuing all goals of primary science education. The contribution to observation of class discussion is illustrated by an example of six and seven year olds who were bubbling over to tell what they had seen following a session observing mealworms. The discussion could easily have been disorganized, with comments on various aspects of mealworm structure and behaviour following one another in quick succession. Instead, the teacher kept the subject to the observation made by the first child to report. This concerned the number of legs the mealworms had, and other children were invited to add comments about this while new topics were kept at bay. There was a considerable bonus in doing this since it emerged that some children thought the mealworms had 3 legs, others that they had 6 legs and others claimed to have seen 8 legs. So this discussion turned out to be a considerable stimulus to further observation, focused on this particular point, and the observations made were far more detailed and accurate than on the first occasion.

Extending knowledge

For this purpose, where teachers wish children to take notice of some specific changes or details, there has to be some framework provided in which observation takes place. Three particularly useful ways of providing the framework are through drawing, discussion, and defining questions to be answered by investigation.

Drawing has a time-honoured role in encouraging observation and knowledge of the objects shown. Some have cast doubt on whether this reputation is justified and certainly it should not be assumed that the act of drawing something will of itself increase knowledge (see Chapter 8). But the task can be presented in various ways. For example, before some children were sent out to observe grasshoppers, their teacher asked them to try to draw a grasshopper from memory as well as they could. As soon as they began, they realized what they did not know about grasshoppers and so they eagerly took the opportunity to find out these things from observation.

Discussion can be used to serve the same function in a group as drawing does on an individual basis, that is, to heighten awareness of what information they can obtain by observation. A class being taken to visit a church with particular interest in the signs of age and weathering of stone was prepared beforehand by a discussion in which the teacher asked them where they thought the stone would be most worn, how they would recognize weathering and wearing away, in what ways did they think old stone would differ from newer stones and so on. There was not necessarily agreement on any of these points and this increased the children's interest in going to see for themselves. They made observations which almost certainly would not have been made without the focusing effect of the discussion.

Questions for investigation, as discussed in Chapter 6, can be expressed as a broad problem or in a form which indicates the kinds of observations which might be made. The question 'What difference does hot water make when sugar is dissolved?' leaves open the decision as to what observations to make. 'Does sugar dissolve faster in hot water than in cold water?' directs observation to the time taken for sugar to dissolve. When starting from the broader problems, children may need help to consider the observations which might be relevant to the investigation. Many 'What happens if . . .' questions benefit from treatment in this way. Take 'What happens if we make pancakes with self-raising flour instead of plain flour?' Without any discussion it is likely that the children will look for differences between the pancakes made with different flours only at the end of the exercise – in the taste, probably. With some initial discussion, though, they may be alerted to look for differences in the events, at each stage in the making. So the two mixtures will be made simultaneously and observations made during mixing of the ingredients, immediately before cooking, during cooking and after cooking. In this way they will more likely come to a realization of the part played by raising agents in the cooking process through seeing the bubbles appearing in the mixture made with self-raising flour when it is heated.

Stimulating investigation

A short period of free observation or of free play with the materials is a most effective way of stimulating children to raise questions, to wonder about things. The period allowed should not be too long; some recent research (Symington, 1981) has suggested that ten minutes is sufficient. It has also been found that the materials provided have a considerable effect and should be chosen so that differences among events or objects can be readily observed. Such observations automatically lead to questions being raised about why there are differences. For instance, if children are given a simple pendulum, a bob on a string, but only one, they will not necessarily observe that the number of swings in a certain time can vary. However, if the children are provided with two pendulums, differing in lengths of string and weight of bob, then they are almost certain to note that one swings more quickly than the other. Consequently they begin to raise questions as to whether the difference is because of the string, the bob or both.

Drawing conclusions

Conclusions generally concern relationships and as such are abstract. The observations from which they are drawn are the concrete instances which are bound together in the conclusion. The link between the concrete instance and the abstraction must never be lost by premature generalization. The teacher has to make sure that the children grasp the link and see the conclusion as a neat way of summarizing the results, not as something separate from them. It helps to discuss with them the consequences of the conclusions or generalizations they offer, at the time when these can be checked by observation. So, for example, if some children are convinced that the mass of the pendulum bob *does* make a difference, they should be asked for a prediction about how they expect a pendulum with a bob of greater mass to behave and then encouraged to try it. If this bob also has a different size than the ones of less mass, they might be challenged to investigate this variable. Similarly, if they conclude that condensation appears on objects which are very cold, they might be asked to say if it would appear on a given surface which is at room temperature. They should then try to make water condense on it to see if their conclusion holds. In such ways further observations are made which help children in reaching more powerful conclusions. At the same time they may appreciate something else about conclusions, that they should always be regarded as tentative and can be changed when new evidence appears.

The teacher's questioning, too, should not come only at the end of an investigation (see Chapter 4). Ideally the teacher should be observing how the children carry out their enquiry, but she cannot be in several places at once. Inevitably when she comes to talk with a group about how they are progressing she will not know whether certain details, which may be critical, have been observed. The questioning should then in the first instance be aimed at a recapitulation of the evidence gathered. If unexpected results are reported, the teacher should ask for a replay without suggesting that what the children have said is 'wrong'. Take the case of the group measuring the relative strength of threads of different kinds. They told the teacher that the thickness of the thread made no difference to the strength. To the question, 'Tell me how you dediced that?' they replied, 'Well, when we hung 600 grams on the thick one, it broke and the same with the thin one'. In this case imperfect experimental technique prevented them making the observations which the teacher had expected them to make. It often happens that children just do not observe the things we may assume that they have observed. This is because we, as adults, know that the opportunity for the observation is there, but for various reasons what the children have observed may be subtly different.

Summary of main points

Observation is an important means by which we gather information about the world around us. It is a skill which can be, and needs to be, developed by children so that they can more effectively learn directly from the objects and materials around them. The value for the children of developing skills in observation is not to be judged in terms of whether they *can* observe more effectively, but whether they *do* and in doing so become more effective in grasping concepts, in gathering information, in proposing investigations and in drawing conclusions from them. Evidence has been quoted to show that children's observation skills are underused; children are capable of seeing detail and detecting sequences in events, but often fail to notice these things unless they are pointed out. This adds force to the point that observation is not the same as using the senses; what we take in is influenced by existing ideas, expectations and how we view a particular task.

Some of the roles which observation plays in learning have been described: in contributing to concept development, in extending knowledge, in stimulating investigation and in helping to arrive at conclusions from investigations. Actions which teachers might consider to ensure that observation skills are developed and do fill these roles can be summarized as follows:

Guidelines for developing observation and promoting its role in learning

1 Always give children sufficient time to observe something; when new material is introduced, allow about ten minutes of free play before starting to discuss or focus observations.

2 After the initial period of observation, as appropriate, give definite guidance to go beyond superficial features and into detail. At times, a focus to observation can be given in the form of a defined task – to draw, to answer questions, to compare particular features.

3 Provide plenty of material for children to handle and observe.

4 Give thought to the selection of materials so that, by observation, children are able to find differences and similarities, sequences in events and evidence on which to base tentative conclusions.

5 Organize observation activities so that children can talk in groups about what they find.

6 Organize whole-class discussions in which groups or individuals tell each other what they have observed.

7 Sometimes provide a stimulus for observation by discussing events or objects *beforehand* so that the children are ready to look out for certain kinds of evidence or information (particularly relevant when observation time is limited, as on a visit).

8 Take care in deciding the kind of question to pose as a stimulus to children's observation; broadly focused questions have the merit of allowing children to decide for themselves what to observe but narrowly focused ones have their place in cases where there is something special that the children might miss.

4 The right question at the right time

Jos Elstgeest

A child was reflecting sunlight onto the wall with a mirror. The teacher asked: 'Why does the mirror reflect sunlight?' The child had no way of knowing, felt bad about it and learned nothing. Had the teacher asked, 'What do you get when you stand twice as far away from the wall?', the child would have responded by doing just that, and would have seen his answer reflected on the wall.

Another teacher took his class out to explore the surroundings. They came to a flower bed with what he called 'four o'clock flowers'. He asked: 'Why do these flowers close in the early evening and open again in the morning?' Nobody, including the teacher, knew. The question came from the 'testing reflex' that we all struggle with. He could have asked: 'Would the same flower that closes at night open again the next morning?' And the children could have labelled some flowers and found out the answers.

I once witnessed a marvellous science lesson virtually go to ruins. It was a class of young secondary school girls who, for the first time, were let free to handle batteries, bulbs and wires. They were busy incessantly, and there were cries of surprise and delight. Arguments were settled by 'You see?', and problems were solved with, 'Let's try!' Hardly a thinkable combination of batteries, bulbs and wires was left untried. Then, in the midst of the hubbub, the teacher clapped her hands and, chalk poised at the blackboard, announced: 'Now, girls, let us summarize what we have learned today. Emmy, what is a battery?' 'Joyce, what is the positive terminal?' 'Lucy, what is the correct way to close a circuit?' And the 'correct' diagram was deftly sketched and labelled, the 'correct' symbols were added, and the 'correct' definitions were scribbled down. And Emmy, Joyce and Lucy and the others deflated audibly into silence and submission, obediently copying the diagram and the summary. What they had done seemed of no importance. The questions were in no way related to their work. The rich experience with the batteries and other equipment, which would have given them plenty to talk and think about and to question, was in no way used to bring order and system into the information they actually did gather.

These teachers were asking the 'wrong' questions, ones which were unproductive in encouraging the children's learning. But how does the teacher diagnose such a question?

What is a 'wrong' question?

Wrong questions tend to begin with such innocent interrogatives as why, how or what. But this is deceptive, for many good questions, too, begin with similar expressions. The real character of wrong questions lies in their 'wordiness'. They are purely verbal questions which require wordy answers, often neatly dressed in bookish phrases. Generally the answers precede the questions and are to be found in textbooks. They can also be obtained from blackboards and preserved in copybooks. When, therefore, a wordy question is asked, children try to look for the words of the answer and are totally lost when they cannot be found. These questions are not problems to be solved. They draw away from scientific problem solving.

However, recognizing a 'wrong' question is one thing, how to ascertain a 'right' question is quite another. For what is a good question? A good question is the first step towards an answer; is a problem to which there is a solution. A good question is a stimulating question which is an invitation to a closer look, a new experiment or a fresh exercise. The right question leads to where the answer can be found: to the real objects or events under study, there where the solution lies hidden. The right question asks children to show rather than to say the answer: they can go and make sure for themselves. I would like to call such questions 'productive' questions, because they stimulate productive activity. There are productive questions of various sorts. In the course of a scientific study they usually follow a certain pattern, since the 'answerability' of one type of question depends on experience obtained through endeavouring to answer questions of another kind.

Attention-focusing questions

The simplest kind of productive question is the straightforward 'have you seen', or 'do you notice' type of question. These are sometimes indispensible, in order to fix attention on some significant detail which might easily be overlooked. Children frequently take care of these questions themselves by their constant exclamations of 'Look here!', so the teacher need not always bother. Children ask these questions at all times but particularly at the introduction of new objects of study. The necessary initial exploration of new materials, the 'messing about' and 'getting to know you' stage of exploration, is very much a 'can you see and do you notice' situation. The 'what?' questions closely follow, of course. 'What is it?' 'What does it do?' 'What does it show about itself?' 'What happens?' 'What do I find inside (outside)?' 'What do I see, feel, hear?' And simple observation is the route to the first simple answers, followed by more complicated questions.

Measuring and counting questions

Questions such as 'how many?', 'how long?' and 'how often?', are measuring and counting questions to which the children can check their answers themselves. They can use new skills, learn to use new instruments, and feel confident, for no teacher can challenge your measuring ruler. There are many situations in which these questions arise, and they lead naturally to the next category of questions: comparison questions. 'Is it longer, stronger, heavier, more?' These are comparison questions and there are many ways of phrasing them. Often they are preceded by 'how much?', which adds a quantitative aspect and necessitates greater accuracy.

Comparison questions

Other, more qualitative, comparison questions bring about sharper observation. For instance: 'In how many ways are your seeds alike and how do they differ?' Things can differ in many respects, such as in shape, colour, size, texture, structure, markings and so forth. Carefully phrased comparison questions help children to bring order into chaos and unity in variety. Classifying, attribute games, making identification keys, or making tables of collected data, are disguised comparison questions. These questions logically lead to another class of questions which make the children create a different situation, or environment, so they may expect to obtain a different result.

Action questions

These are the 'what happens if' questions which can always be truthfully answered. They entail simple experimentation and never fail to provide a result. They are productive questions of great value and particularly appropriate at the beginning of a scientific study to explore the properties of unfamiliar materials, living or non-living, of forces at work, and of small events taking place.

What happens if you place your antlion in damp sand?
What happens if you pinch the seedleaves off a young growing plant?
What happens if you place a cutting or twig in water?
What happens if you put your twig upside-down?
What happens if you hold your magnet near a match?
What happens if you throw a tiny piece of paper in a spider's web?
Innumerable good examples of 'what happens if . . .' problems can be given which lead to as many solutions that can be readily found to the satisfaction of the children and their teachers.

Working on 'what happens if' problems, children are bound to discover some form of relationship between what they do and the reaction of the thing they handle. This greatly adds to the store of experiences which young children require. As adults, we often assume that children can fill the generalizations and abstractions which we so casually throw around, but children must collect the 'fillings' themselves. An exciting addition to solving 'what happens if' problems is the challenge to predict the outcome. Initially the children will just guess, and find themselves way out in their predictions, but with the accumulation of experiences they become sharper. The ability to predict is a prerequisite to the ability to tackle real or, rather, more complicated problem-solving questions.

Problem-posing questions

After sufficient activities provoked by the type of questions just described, children become ready for a new type of question: the more sophisticated 'can you find a way to' question. This will always set up a real problem-solving situation to which children enthusiastically respond, provided it makes sense to them.

I once asked a class of children, 'Can you make your plant grow sideways?' For a short time they had been studying plants growing in tins, pots, boxes and other contraptions made of plastic bags. I was just a little too anxious and too hasty and, quite rightly, I got the answer, 'No, we cannot'. So we patiently continued with scores of 'what happens if' experiments. Plants were placed in wet and dry conditions, in dark and in light corners, in big boxes and in cupboards, inside collars of white and black paper, upside down, on their side, and in various combinations of these. In other words, the children really made it 'difficult and confusing' for the plants. Their plants, however, never failed to respond in one way or another, and slowly the children began to realize that there was a relationship between the plant and its environment which they controlled. Noticing the ways in which the plants responded, the children became aware that they could somehow control the growth of plants in certain ways, because the responses of the plants became evident by the way they grew. Tips curved upwards, stems bent, plants grew tall and thin, or sometimes withered altogether. The children discovered that moisture as well as light and position has an effect upon the growth of plants.

When the question 'Can you find a way to make your plant grow sideways?' reappeared later there was not only a confident reaction, there was also a good variety of attempts, all sensible, all based on newly acquired experience, and all original. Some children laid their plant on its side and rolled a newspaper tube around the container and the plant. Others manufactured a stand to hold a horizontal tube into which they pushed the top of their plant, (this one turned back). One group closed their plant inside a box with a hole, but they fixed a tube in the hole and directed it towards the light of the class window. Some just tied their plant sideways along a cross stick and added restricting strings as soon as the growing tip curled upward again.

It is obvious that 'can you find a way to . . .' questions must be preceded by a satisfactory exploration of the materials with which the children work. They need to investigate first what possibilities and impossibilities there are, and become familiar with some of the properties of the objects under study particularly those properties which show up in interaction with (things out of) the environment. Source books and teacher's guides can never indicate when the children are ready for more formal, more complicated, problem solving. This is a matter to be decided either by the children themselves when they spontaneously begin to tackle such problems, or by the sound judgement of the teacher when he has sufficient evidence that the children can move on to more sophisticated activities. This is important to note, for if a teacher rigidly adheres to a (necessarily limited) outline in some textbook, there is a good chance that the children will get confused, and the class end in chaos.

The 'can you find a way to' question comes in many guises. 'Can you make a mealworm turn around?' 'Can you make a sinking object float?' 'Can you separate salt from water?' It is in essence a prediction question, a more complicated 'what happens if' question turned around. Finding the solution necessitates the forming of a simple hypothesis and consequent verification in a very direct manner. The acknowledgement of the need to recognize variables and to control these emerges naturally. And this is the point where children's science begins to make real progress.

Teachers' how and why questions

Finally there follows a category of questions which we should approach with caution, as there is a serious danger of misusing them. They are, what I call, 'reasoning' questions and they often ask for some sort of explanation. Naturally these questions tend to start with how and why, and that is where the danger lies. The anxious teacher might want to let himself loose in worthy but wordy explanations which will not be rooted in the children's experience. Anxious children might easily mistake them for test questions to which, they often feel, they should have been given model answers. The lack of a model answer makes children afraid to be 'wrong'. But 'reasoning' questions are very important in science education and we should never eliminate them. After all, every youngster is a born how and why questioner, so how could we avoid them? What we should eliminate however is the impression that to every question of this sort there is one right answer. Reasoning questions are not meant to be answered in a unique way. They are meant to make children think and reason independently about their own experiences. They are meant to make them reflect upon the relationships they have discovered or recognized, so they can carefully begin to draw conclusions, or make generalizations, on the strength of real evidence that they have collected or uncovered. These questions are intended to open up discussion, to make children freely express what and how they think about their observations and findings. The discussion, the dialogue, the sharing of ideas helps in recognizing new relationships and it aids understanding. It is essential that the children talk freely, that they are not held back by any red light of fear, for even the most preposterous statement can provoke argument, and argument leads to correction, provided it is based on found, and sound, evidence.

A child can more easily take responsibility for his answer if the question is presented with the little addition: 'Why, do you think ...?' In that case even though there may be something wrong with the thinking and the opinion may be subjected to fierce argument, the answer to the question will always be right. The child, after all, knows best what he thinks. (The same advice and more is given in Harlen, Darwin and Murphy, 1977.) Care is not only needed in how these questions are phrased, but also in when they are presented. Children who are working with mosquito larvae for the first time may be effectively put off from further exploration and thought by a premature 'Why do the larvae come to the surface of the water?' How would they know? They may have framed this question themselves, which is a sign that they do not know, so why ask them?

However, it may well happen that children have watched mosquito larvae wriggle down to the bottom, time after time, whenever they were disturbed by a waving hand, or by a knock on the jar that contained them, or by shaking or stirring the water in which they swam. These children would also see the larvae come up again and again; they might notice their tail tubes sticking up just above the surface of the water. They may time how long the larvae can stay under the water surface. Whenever the larvae come up, the children can discourage them from doing so by shaking the jar, or by knocking the sides of it. And what would the larvae do it you cover the surface of the water with snippets of paper or a sheet of cellophane? The children are bound to become aware of the larvae's persistence to reach the surface. Only after these and similar experiences can the children become involved in a sensible argument when asked, 'Why do you think these larvae come up to the surface of the water?' In the first place, the 'why', here, is easily translated into 'what for'. Secondly, the children can now express their thoughts with confidence, because they have something to think and to talk about, all based on a series of common experiences to which they can refer. They produce relevant evidence. Within the same frame of reference the teacher can now take part in the discussion as an equal. This is important, for the answer 'they come up to breathe' is by no means an obvious one. Many water creatures never come up to breathe, and a tail is not readily associated with the act of breathing. Yet the teacher's contribution may point in the direction of respirational need without it becoming, for the children, an act of faith.

Children's how and why questions

There are a few more aspects of the 'why' question which are useful to consider here. We cannot avoid the questions the children ask, and they often ask 'why?'. The erroneous, though flattering, attitude of many parents and children tempts teachers often to bluff their way out with vague, exalted, impressive-sounding 'answers', but this does not help the children. Of course, within their experience they can be given answers which point out relationships, but the experience is not always present. Breaking up the question into manageable 'what happens if' questions and 'let us see how' observations may try the children's patience, but will provide necessary experiences to make understanding possible. In any case, it is good science education.

Nevertheless, real difficulties can arise, for there are many 'why' questions which simply have never been answered yet; others cannot even be answered by science. For instance, questions about why things are as they are lead us rapidly into the realm of metaphysics or theology or mythology. Worthy answers can be obtained, but these are to be found beyond science, and this should be made clear. But also within the bounds of human science there remain many questions yet unanswered, and even more to which the humble but honest teacher must admit, 'I do not know'. Well, do admit it, for this is a healthy lesson to the children. Science is the search for, rather than the answer to, our questions of why and how. Besides, both 'why' and 'how' are illusive questions. As soon as we approach a satisfying answer, we become aware of a new problem, and a fresh 'why' or 'how' shimmers above the horizon. We have not yet reached the final answer, to a single final 'why?' or 'how?', so the search continues, and it is into this search that we introduce our children. A great number of why-questions are by nature queries of 'what for?', 'to what purpose?' or 'where to?' and these refer to structure–function relationships. Other why questions search for cause–effect relationships, or ask for why things behave the way they do. The teacher's attempt to break these questions up into simpler questions reveals their true nature, and the search for solutions begins to alternate between doing and reasoning.

The simple 'becauses' reasoned out by the children themselves on the strength of their own evidence and their own experiences are far more valuable and important than any of the reasons provided by adults and faultlessly recited without understanding. Even an adult's understanding depends on his own step-by-step progress through masses of experiences, and many of us have understood things, that we were supposed to have learned at school, only years after we were set free to educate ourselves.

Teachers' explanations

Children may be interested in solving problems that are beyond their scope, either because the necessary equipment is inadequate (or not refined enough) or because the required experimentation is simply too difficult or complicated. A knowledgeable teacher is then a great asset and can contribute considerably toward widening the children's horizon of learning and knowledge, because this teacher can fathom the depth of the children's ability and thus measure the quality and quantity of the information or explanation to be given. When children ask, they indicate that they want to know, and when they want to know, they are interested. Interest is a fertile ground in which the teacher's explanation is gratefully and fruitfully accepted. The clever teacher also recognizes that, where questions arise and interest is present, functional literacy shows its worth. Children will be led to good books. Not only will they look for and find an answer to their problem, they will also find that other scientists have grappled with such a problem, and often they may appreciate how much effort and research was required in order to find a solution.

Summary of main points

A question already has within it the kind of answer that can be given, even before it is spoken. There are many different kinds of question and their varying effect on children is striking. The purpose of teachers' questions should be to promote children's activity and reasoning. Questions which do *not* do this (unproductive questions) are those which ask only about knowledge of words, often for repetition of words given earlier by the teacher or to be found in a book.

Questions which encourage activity (productive questions) come in various kinds and form a hierarchy reflecting the experience of the children.

Questions which promote reasoning often start with 'why' or 'how' and can be asked by both teacher and class. It has been suggested that teachers' why questions should include the phrase 'why, do *you* think', and should be carefully timed so that children have the necessary experience to form a view which is genuinely their own.

Children's why questions often present problems for a teacher, for not all can be answered and not all should be answered. Some ask about relationships that children can discuss; these can be turned into productive questions (see also Chapter 5). The points emerging so far lead to these guidelines.

Guidelines for 'productive' questions

1 Study the effect on children of asking different kinds of question so that you can distinguish the 'productive' from the 'unproductive'.
2 Use the simplest form of productive question (attention-focusing) during initial exploration to help children take note of details that they might overlook.
3 Use measuring and counting questions to nudge children from purely qualitative observation towards quantitative observation.
4 Use comparison questions to help children order their observations and data.
5 Use action questions to encourage experimentation and the investigation of relationships.
6 Use problem-posing questions when children are capable of setting up for themselves hypotheses and situations to test them.
7 Choose the type of question to suit the children's experience in relation to the particular subject of enquiry.

Guidelines for 'why' and 'how' questions

1 When asking questions to stimulate children's reasoning, make sure they include 'what do you think about' or 'why do you think'.
2 Don't ask questions of this type until children have had the necessary experience they need so that they can reason from evidence.
3 When children ask 'why' questions consider whether they have the experience to understand the answer.
4 Don't be afraid to say you don't know an answer, or that no one knows (if it is a philosophical question).

5 Break up questions whose answers would be too complex into ones that concern relationships the children can find out about and understand.
6 Take children's questions seriously, as an expression of what interests them; even if the questions cannot be answered, don't discourage the asking.

5 Helping children raise questions – and answering them
Sheila Jelly

In my experience, many of the questions children ask spontaneously are not profitable starting points for science. The commonest questions I get asked in infant classrooms are along the lines, 'Is Mr Jelly your husband/father/brother?' I quote this not as a facetious example, but to make the point that questions from young children reflect an urge to make associations with their previous experience. Even when this associative process is triggered by interesting materials with great potential for scientific investigation, a child's curiosity often does not show itself as spontaneous questioning but rather as a statement of interests. 'Look it (snail) has little eyes on stalks'. In situations like this, teachers have to intervene in order to frame problems that children can investigate in a scientific way: 'Are they really eyes?' 'Can snails see?' 'How might we find out?' So in practice it is very often a *teacher*'s questioning, not a child's that initiates scientific activity. For this reason any consideration of handling children's questions in science must be closely related to the way in which a teacher handles her own questioning.

In Chapter 4 a series of different types of question were discussed. They were called *productive* because 'they stimulate productive activity' and were distinguished from unproductive questions, which do not lead to scientific activity but the recall of factual knowledge. Unproductive questions are those to which a child either knows the answer ('Where did you find it?') or, if he does not ('What's it called?'), he obtains it from secondary sources – the teacher or books. Such questions may be very useful for encouraging conversation or, with the development of reading skills in mind, for sending children to books to acquire information, but as starting points for scientific activity they are very limited and unproductive. The features of these two types of question are summarized in the table below.

Unproductive	Productive
Promote science as information	Promote science as a way of working
Answers derived from secondary sources by talking/reading	Answers derived from first-hand experience involving practical action with materials
Tend to emphasize answering as the achievement of a correct end product (the right answer)	Encourage awareness that varied answers may each be 'correct' in its own terms and view achievement as what is learnt in the process of arriving at an answer
Successful answering is most readily achieved by verbally fluent children who have confidence and facility with words	Successful answering is achievable by all children

Productive questions are the type we need to encourage in the classroom if we wish to promote science as a way of working, but experience shows that teachers ask far more unproductive questions than productive ones and, frequently find the framing of productive questions a difficult task. This is not at all surprising because most of us have acquired our formal education in bookish environments and have accordingly established questioning styles that tend to require factual answers. But it is important to make the effort to change the pattern of questioning, since productive questions are a very powerful tool for the teacher. They have considerable value when planning science work; they are extremely useful in those 'thinking on the feet' situations where we make an instantaneous response to something a child says or does, and importantly, they are the kind of question that children can profitably 'catch' if we wish them to find their own problems for investigation.

If we are to improve the range and quality of questioning in a classroom three things are required:

1 Improve our own ability to ask questions.
2 Establish a climate of curiosity and questioning that is conducive to question-asking by the children.
3 Develop strategies for handling children's spontaneous questions.

Improving teachers' own questioning skills

From the various types of productive question illustrated in Chapter 4 (see also Chapter 6), it is possible to see that there are general frameworks which can be applied in a variety of situations:

'Which _____ is best for _____?'
'Who has the _____?' (strongest hair, best sight, keenest hearing)
'Will it _____ if we _____?' (swing more quickly if we make it longer)
'Do _____ prefer _____?' (any animal/any food or condition)

The key to generating specific questions for particular situations is *practice*. With this in mind here are three activities for teachers to help improve questioning skills.

1 Try taping conversation when there is science work going on in the classroom. Later analyse the questions the teacher asks. Are they unproductive or productive? What is the proportion of each type? Of the productive questions what kind of child activity did each promote? This is a salutory experience for us all! The first analysis may well prove a little disheartening but, over time, it becomes very encouraging to note how questioning styles can alter.

2 Scrutinize the questions posed in primary science books. Are they unproductive or productive? If productive, what scientific experiences are they encouraging? Many teachers who have carried out this activity report an increased awareness of question types and an increased facility in generating their own productive questions.

3 Use odd moments to practise question-finding. Suppose, for example, you are waiting in a car park (a useful situation, since all schools will have one). What is its potential for science? What productive questions could you ask about it to stimulate children's scientific activity? Make a list of attention-focusing questions (see Chapter 4, p. 37). Try to go beyond the obvious properties such as colour/shape/size/kind/age and include questions involving patterns and relationships. For example:

Which of the cars are rusting?
Which parts of a car rust?
Which parts have no rust?
Do all cars rust in the same place?
Is there any connection between the amount of rust and the age of a car?
What attention-focusing questions might you ask about car tyres, windows or lights?

Try also to identify problem-posing questions (see Chapter 4, p. 39), such as which colour is the best safety colour for a car?' Can you think of others? What productive questions are appropriate for a study of the buildings around the car park?

It's also useful to apply question-finding practice to normal classroom events. Think, for example, of the water play area of an infant classroom. The children will have observational experience of things that float and things that sink. How might their work be extended to involve fair-testing experience? What questions could they be asked? 'Who can make the best boat?' is one that can promote interesting discussion and activity. Can you think of another?

Establishing a classroom climate conducive to children's question-asking

If questioning styles are not taught, a teacher's verbal questioning will probably be the most important factor in establishing a climate conducive to question-asking by children. But it is not the only factor and so it is useful to consider ways by which curiosity might be aroused and how such curiosity can be linked to particular questioning frameworks. As a first step we need to get children's interest stimulated and this means giving them direct contact with materials. It also means that we need to think carefully about the nature of the materials that make children curious. Materials brought in spontaneously by the children have a built-in curiosity factor and need no further discussion; but what of materials selected by teachers? These can usefully be considered in two categories: those with immediate appeal and those that are commonplace when seen through childs' eyes, but which can evoke curiosity if teacher tactics present them in a new and challenging light. The first kind present fewest problems because we know that certain properties such as colour, shape and movement can, in themselves, trigger curiosity. Indeed we constantly capitalize on these facts when we introduce materials into the classroom. But if we remember that children's response is shaped largely by what they guess to be the expectations their teacher has for them, then in many classes materials will promote activities of the kind summarized in Fig. 5.1.

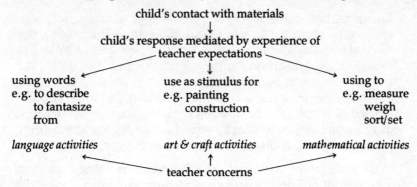

Fig. 5.1

Not surprisingly, therefore, a child's response tends to show itself as an application of the known (procedures and techniques), rather than in a concern for the unknown and an associated generation of questions. For this reason it is helpful to concentrate consciously on building up what we might call the questioning dimension in childrens' expectations of how teacher would like them to respond. This dimension can be developed when they associate with a teacher's productive questioning style. It can also be strengthened by teacher-promoted activities which reinforce the style; activities that bring children into contact with materials linked to appropriate questions, and activities that provide opportunities for children to frame their own productive questions. Increased contact with appropriate questions can be achieved in a variety of ways. For example:

1 By making sure that displays and collections have associated enquiry questions for the children to read, ponder and perhaps explore incidentally to the main work of the class.
2 By introducing a problem corner or a 'question of the week' activity where materials and associated questions are on offer to the children as a stimulus to thought and action which might be incorporated into classwork.
3 By making 'questions to investigate' lists that can be linked to popular information books.
4 By ensuring that in any teacher-made science work cards there is a question framed to encourage children to see their work as enquiry-based and which also provides a useful heading for any resultant work displayed in the classroom.

Opportunities for children to frame productive questions include activities such as:

1 Using regular class time (such as news time or equivalent) to encourage children to talk about something interesting they have observed, and to tell others of the questions it prompts.
2 Encouraging children to supply 'questions of the week' (as in the activity described above).
3 Establishing procedures by which children, having completed a piece of work, are encouraged to list further questions about it. For example, individually when completing a work card or collectively when discussing work on display.

With techniques such as these it is often surprising how much the quality of children's questioning improves over a period of time. However, it should be stated that, initially, most children find it a very difficult task and tend to ask only unproductive questions. They will need lots of encouragement and quite clearly too much emphasis on question-asking too soon can be counter-productive and may result in a 'not another question' dismissal rather than the excitement and enthusiasm we wish to develop.

Curiously, materials that are very 'ordinary' in childrens' eyes often generate more sustained question-asking than materials with obvious child appeal. Perhaps this is because a child's particular involvement with things with immediate appeal is sufficient satisfaction in itself and further scrutiny becomes an intrusive and unwanted distraction. Whatever the reason, it is worth considering how commonplace things can be used to promote question-generating situations. For example:

1 By using collections of everyday things as a focus for linking materials with teacher-framed questions. A collection of kitchen utensils, say, has little immediate appeal but associated with appropriate questions it can provide challenging involvement. If for example the tools are sorted by function many enquiry questions can follow. In time, children can be encouraged to organize their own collections of 'ordinary' things and supply questions for others to investigate.
2 By selecting materials for practical investigation that do unexpected things. As for example, the effect of dropping a plasticine ball on polystyrene when investigating bouncing balls, Anomolous happenings are very good question stimulators.
3 By using magnifiers and microscopes to extend children's observation so that they will see exciting detail in familiar things.
4 By considering the extent to which the conventional aesthetic approach to display can be broadened to include materials

which may not be visually pleasing but which justify inclusion in display themes because of their potential for enquiry work. For example, a display centred on the theme of the sea is made richer educationally by the inclusion of some tatty, ugly shoreline debris if the material is linked to challenging questions.

Teacher tactics of the kind described do, undoubtedly, improve the climate of enquiry in a classroom and, as a consequence, lead to more spontaneous questioning by children.

Handling children's spontaneous questions

Spontaneous questions from children come in various forms and carry a variety of meanings. Consider for example the following questions. How would you respond to each?

1 What is a baby tiger called?
2 What makes it rain?
3 Why can you see yourself in a window?
4 Why is the hamster ill?
5 If I mix these (paints), what colour will I get?
6 If God made the world, who made God?
7 How long do cows live?
8 How does a computer work?
9 When will the tadpoles be frogs?
10 Are there people in outer space?

Clearly the nature of each question shapes our response to it. Even assuming we wanted to give children the correct answers, we could not do so in all cases. Question 6 has no answer, but we can of course respond to it. Question 10 is similar; it has no certain answer but we could provide a conjectural one based on some relevant evidence. All the other questions do have answers, but this does not mean that each answer is similar in kind, nor does it mean that all answers are known to the teacher, nor are all answers equally accessible to children.

When we analyse what we do everyday as part of our stock in-trade, namely respond to children's questions, we encounter a highly complex situation. Not only do questions vary in kind, requiring answers that differ in kind, but children also have different reasons for asking a question. The question may mean 'I want a direct answer', it might mean 'I've asked the question to show you I'm interested but I'm not after a literal answer.' Or, it could mean, 'I've asked the question because I want your attention – the answer is not important.' Given all these variables how then should we handle the questions raised spontaneously in science work? The comment of one teacher is pertinent here:

'The children's questions worry me. I can deal with the child who just wants attention, but because I've no science background I take other questions at face value and get bothered when I don't know the answer. I don't mind saying I don't know, though I don't want to do it too often. I've tried the "let's find out together" approach, but its not easy and can be very frustrating.'

Many teachers will identify with these remarks and what follows is a suggested strategy for those in a similar position. Its not the only strategy possible, nor is it completely fail safe, but it has helped a large number of teachers deal with difficult questions. By difficult questions I mean those that require complex information and/or explanation for a full answer. The approach does not apply to simple informational questions such as 1, 7 and 9 on the list above because these are easy to handle, either by telling or by reference to books, or expertise, in ways familiar to the children in other subject areas. Nor is it relevant to spontaneous questions of the productive kind discussed earlier, because these can be answered by doing. Essentially it is a strategy for handling complex questions and in particular those of the 'why' kind that are the most frequent of all spontaneous questions. They are difficult questions because they carry an apparent request for a full explanation which may not be known to the teacher and, in any case, is likely to be conceptionally beyond a child's understanding.

The strategy recommended is one that turns the question to practical action with a 'let's see what we can do to understand more' approach. The teaching skill involved is the ability to 'turn' the question. Consider, for example, a situation in which children are exploring the properties of fabrics. They have dropped water on different types and become fascinated by the fact that water stays 'like a little ball' on felt. They tilt the felt, rolling the ball around, and someone asks 'Why is it like a ball?'. How might the question be turned by applying the 'doing more to understand' approach? We need to analyse the situation quickly and use what I call a 'variables scan'. The explanation must relate to something 'going on' between the water and the felt surface so causing the ball. That being so, ideas for childrens activities will come if we consider ways in which the situation could be varied to better understand the making of the ball. We could explore surfaces keeping the drop the same, and explore drops keeping the surface the same. These thoughts can prompt others that bring ideas nearer to what children might do. For example:

1 Focusing on the surface, keeping the drop the same:
    What is special about the felt that helps make the ball?
    Which fabrics are good 'ball-makers'?
    Which are poor?
    What have the good ball-making fabrics in common?
    What surfaces are good ball-makers?
    What properties do these share with the good ball-making fabrics?
    Can we turn the felt into a poor ball-maker?
2 Focusing on the water drop, keeping the surface the same:
    Are all fluids good ball-makers?
    Can we turn the water into a poor ball-maker?

Notice how the 'variables scan' results in the development of productive questions that can be explored by the children. The original question has been turned to practical activity and children exploring along these lines will certainly enlarge their understanding of what is involved in the phenomenon. They will not arrive at a detailed explanation but may be led towards simple generalization of their experience, such as 'A ball will form when . . .' or 'It will not form when . . .'.

Some teachers see the strategy as one of diversion (which it is) and are uneasy that the original question remains unanswered, but does this matter? The question has promoted worthwhile scientific enquiry and we must remember that its meaning for the child may well have been 'I'm asking it to communicate my interest'. For such children interest has certainly been developed and children who may have initiated the question as a request for explanation in practice, are normally satisfied by the work their question generates.

The strategy can be summarized as follows:

Analyse the question
↓
Consider if it can be 'turned'
to practical activity (with its
'real' materials or by simulating them)
↓
Carry out a 'variables scan' and identify
productive questions
↓
Use questions to promote activity
↓
Consider simple generalization children
might make *from experience*

It is not a blueprint for handling *all* difficult questions, but it does provide a framework that helps us to cope with many of them. Its use becomes easier with practice. Try using it to respond to question 3 on page 53 (a comparatively simple application) and to the question, 'Why do aeroplanes stay up?' which is a more complex application. The task may be difficult initially, indeed several aspects of the analysis and use of questions put forward in this chapter may prove likewise. But the effective handling of questions is vital in any science programme.

Summary of main points

Children learn their question-asking habits from teachers. If children are to be encouraged to raise questions that lead to investigation, this is one more reason (added to those given in Chapter 4) for teachers making the effort to ask more productive questions and fewer unproductive ones. Some specific ways in which teachers can practise and improve question skills have been suggested.

The atmosphere in the classroom must also be conducive to encouraging children to ask questions. Some ways of showing that questions are welcome are by adding questions to displays and collections, introducing a problem corner in the classroom, creating lists of 'questions to investigate', making sure any work cards or sheets are framed in terms of investigable questions. Regular discussion of questions is also important. Children, like teachers, do not find it easy at first to change the emphasis in their questioning from unproductive to productive. Novel materials are not necessarily the best stimulus; often more familiar ones help children raise questions, especially with a lead from the teacher to the kind of productive questions that can be asked.

Once children begin to ask questions they will ask ones of all kinds; some will be difficult for teachers to handle, but it is important to find a way of doing this which does not make the child wish (s)he had not asked. A strategy has been described for analysing children's questions so that unproductive ones can be used productively.

Guidelines for encouraging children's questioning

1 Provide a wide range of materials for children to respond to.
2 Practise and improve your questioning style so that it provides an example for the children.
3 Provide a climate of enquiry for children to work in.

4 Encourage children to form and to discuss their own questions.
5 Respond positively to children's spontaneous questions.
6 Turn children's unproductive questions into productive ones that promote investigation of real materials.

6 Helping children to plan investigations

Wynne Harlen

What is involved in planning an investigation? Here are some plans written by 10 to 11 year olds in attempting to describe what test they would do to find out if their finger nails grew faster than their toe nails. These quotations are the complete answers of the children concerned with the original spelling and punctuation preserved.

Brian: To describe it it would cut my nails right down and see which ones would grow first the quickest thats how I would do it.

Lisa: You could keep checking your finger nails and toe nails for a week and keep all your infamation on a block chart then at the end of the week you can see which grows faster.

Leroy: My test would be I would cut my finger nails and I would cut my toe nails and in a week or two I would see how long they have grown and if my toe nails are longer they grow faster.

John: I would measure them each day to see which had grown faster.

Candy: At the begining of a 2 week period I would measure the length of my toe nails and I would also measure the length of my finger nails. At the end of the 2 weeks I would measure them both again and I would then know if my toe nails grow faster than my finger nails by taking the measurement of the beging of the two weeks from the measurement at the end of the two weeks.

As these were written plans they are undoubtedly limited by the children's ability to express themselves on paper and we are probably right in supposing that the children could explain what they mean much more precisely in discussion. However, if we take these at face value for the moment, and don't read into them what is not there, it is interesting to see to what extent each contains the important elements of a plan.

At first reading it seems that the general approach of all five children is fairly sound. They all perceive the problem as one of comparison of rates of growth. Measurement seems to be implied, but in fact only John and Candy actually mention measuring something. Brian has not identified what is to be measured at all and has done scarcely more than change 'find out which grows faster' into 'see which ones grow the quickest'. Of course, he may know how 'quickest' would be measured in practice, but we can't tell from what he has written.

Lisa says she would 'keep checking' the nails for a week but does not state that she would 'check' them both at the same time, which would be important for the sort of comparison she has in mind. Lisa and John state that they would be looking for changes from day to day (Brian indicates no time period) although their experience might well have taught them that little measurable change would have taken place in one day. However, by regular measurement they avoid Leroy's pitfall of looking for comparisons at the end of a time without having compared things at the start. Leroy and Candy suggest a period of time of two weeks, which shows application of everyday knowledge to the problem.

In this problem there is no control over the growth of nails (the independent variable) and in this it differs from many investigations where fair comparisons can only be made if the two things being compared are treated similarly. We shall consider some of these kinds of investigations later.

How will they use their results to give an answer to the original problem? Candy states carefully that she would need to subtract one set of measurements from the other; Leroy also says how the result would give the answer (though it would only be a valid result if the nails started at the same length). The others say little on this subject; Lisa's suggestion of a block graph is rather as if it were a magic wand.

There are some essential parts of planning which none of these children include – and which are rare in most children's planning. None suggests the equipment they would need to use. Would a ruler be good enough for measuring the small changes in the length of nails? If they had thought about this they might have rejected the whole idea of direct measurement and perhaps cut pieces of paper to fit the nails and compared these with each other instead. None of the plans suggests making measurement on different toes and fingers to replicate the results, yet they seem prepared to make conclusions from an implied single set of measurements about toe and finger nails in general.

Perhaps this is enough about nails, but certainly enough to show that there is a great deal of thinking – and fun – in working out how to tackle quite a simple problem. Surely one of the important aims of science education is to help children approach problems with this scientific thinking. Planning and carrying out investigations should be closely co-ordinated and in practice the planning often takes place, or at least continues, after an investigation has begun. In considering planning separately it is not being suggested that it is a separate activity. Rather it is a neglected one (see later on page 67) and deserves some consideration in its own right.

The skills involved in planning

Planning concerns the various steps in between raising a question or identifying a problem and supplying an answer. In planning, these steps are thought about and decided rather than carried out in practice. However, the fact that they *are* to be carried out in practice is important to the process, for planning has to be purposeful.

So we start with a problem, which may or may not be expressed as something which can be investigated. If it is not in such a form, the first step is to express it so that it is an investigable question. Several investigable questions might come from one initial problem. For example the question, 'How do we get the best results when we dye our material?' is not in investigable form. Some of the investigable questions could be identified from it are:

Does the strength of dye make any difference to the colour?
Does the time the material is left in the dye make any difference?
Does the type of material make any difference?

Maybe it is only relevant to investigate one of these; in any case they should be considered one at a time. Having selected one, the following stages concern the identification of the things or conditions to be changed (the independent variables), the things or conditions to keep the same (variables to be controlled), the outcome or effects to be looked for (the dependent variable) which give the results. Then some thought has to be given to how the results will be used to answer the original problem.

This may sound rather theoretical, but the following examples should help to show that it is a familiar planning process used when we want to make a 'fair test' of something.

The steps in the process are not necessarily carried out in a set order. The order varies according to the type of problem. The two main types which lead to investigation are 'I wonder what happens if' problems and 'I wonder whether' problems. Generally the former concern problems where a variable can be changed and its effect observed (compare this with 'Action questions' in Chapter 4). The latter usually concern problems where the manipulation of a variable is either not possible (for example, questions about the weather or solar system) or not desirable (life cycles, the working of the inside of the human body).

The problem about the dye led to 'I wonder what happens if' questions. For one such question, about whether the strength affects the colour which is produced, the planning steps are shown below.

Problem	How do we get the best results when dyeing?
Investigable question	What happens to the colour if we change the strength of the dye?
What should be changed in the investigation? (the independent variable)	The amount of dye dissolved
What should be kept the same?	The amount of water, the temperature, the time of soaking, the type of material and any others which might be thought likely to make a difference
What kind of effect should be observed? (the dependent variable)	The colour
How will the result be used to answer the question?	If there is a difference it will be possible to say what change resulted in a deeper or paler colour. If not, the answer will be that changing the strength made no difference in this investigation

So far the planning has been carried out at the level of principle or general strategy. There has been no decision as to how many different strengths of dye will be used, how the other variables will be controlled and how the depth of colour (the dependent variable) will be detected. The plan is not yet in terms of what is to be done, that is, not yet operationalized.

The practical limitations on what can be done have to be taken into account, since it is no use preparing a plan which ignores the fact that, say, spectrometers or high-speed cameras are not available in primary and middle schools. So each step has to be translated into action that can be taken as follows:

Planning step	General plan (not operationalized)	Specific plan (operationalized)
What should be changed?	The amount of dye dissolved	At least three different amounts; try 4 (have we enough dye?)
What should be kept the same?	The water	Measure the amounts, make same in some other way
	The temperature	Use a thermometer or judge by hand
	The type of material	Make sure piece cut from same material
	The time of soaking	Use clock or dye pieces simultaneously
How will a difference in colour be observed?	Compare different pieces of material	If differences are small get several people to judge and perhaps put them in order of palest to deepest

There are usually several ways of putting a general plan into operation and part of the skill of planning is to improvise and to overcome practical obstacles. In the dyeing example the lack of, say, a thermometer, might pose a problem. This could be overcome by mixing all the dyes at the same time using water from the same source and dyeing all the pieces of fabric simultaneously. This obviously has disadvantages in terms of utensils and manpower, but the pros and cons will vary from one classroom to another.

Practical details can often assume such a proportion as to confuse the issue. An important role for the teacher is to make sure this does not happen. It helps in doing this to realize that the various steps in planning are the same from one problem to another. The children will not necessarily realize this, but it is important for the teacher to do so. The general plan is a useful *first* stage in planning; the *second* stage is to translate the general plan into a set of actions to be taken.

Suppose the problem had been about the rate of vibration of a toy suspended from a spring. The general planning is not too difficult. There are several investigable questions associated with this problem and again we take only one.

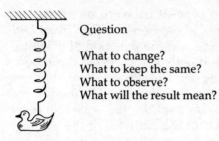

Question	Does the weight of the duck make any difference?
What to change?	The weight on the spring
What to keep the same?	The type of spring, its length
What to observe?	How quickly it bobs up and down
What will the result mean?	If there is a difference in 'bobbing' speed it will be caused by changing the weight on the spring

Fig. 6.1

The second stage of planning will have to take into account what is possible. How many different weights should be tried? Do they have to be toys? As with the dyes there should be at least 3 and ideally 4 or 5 different values to the independent variable (the weight on the spring) if a pattern or relationship is being sought. If the length and type of spring needs to be kept the same, how many identical springs are available? If there are no two springs the same, then the various trials will have to be carried out using the same spring, one after another. This has implications for answering the question 'How to measure or compare how quickly the weight bobs up and down?'. If there is only one spring direct comparison is impossible and some timing device is needed. If there is no timer in working order the problem calls for ingenuity, such as using someone's pulse or digital watch. There is still the question of what to time. Children's suggestions for this have included:

'the time for twenty bobs'
'one minute and count how many bobs it makes'
'time how long it takes to stop bobbing'
'time how long one bob takes'.

These are all worth discussion, which may lead to one or more being eliminated. But if there is not enough evidence to show that one method is clearly better than the others then the alternative methods should be tried. There is not only value from such experience relating to planning future investigations, but also value in terms of applying concepts. The child who would measure the rate of movement in terms of its duration probably has not sorted out these two different concepts in his own mind and the practical experience may give him chance to do so. Note that this opportunity comes only through being able to be involved in the planning himself, not through following instructions to 'time 20 bobs'. This is a point to which further reference will be made later.

Turning now to the second type of problem mentioned on page 61, the 'I wonder whether' ones, here the plan must concern the observations to be made and the selection of evidence. Problems in this category are ones such as 'Does the moon's phase affect our weather?' 'If the daffodils flower early, do all the spring flowers appear earlier too?' 'Is the wood at the top of a tree the same as the wood at the bottom?' In these cases there can be no manipulation of the moon or the daffodils or the wood, in contrast to the way in which the strength of the dye could be changed. Nonetheless the problems can lead to investigable questions and these can be subject to 'fair testing'. Because of the nature of the problem, the planning steps are slightly different from before.

Let us look at the problem of the wood in a tree. This was actually investigated by some children in a school when a tree was felled in the school grounds. The children obviously showed interest in the felling and began to discuss what uses the wood might have. Some said that it would depend which part of the trunk was used because 'the wood at the bottom is harder than the wood at the top'. They thought this should be so because 'the wood at the bottom has to stand all that weight; besides the top wood isn't so old'. Not everyone was satisfied by this argument that there must be a difference, so they wanted to find out. The investigation had to be carefully planned because they had to have wood samples sawn off and they had to decide what the wanted. The steps in planning are shown below.

Problem	Is the wood the same at different points up the trunk?
Investigable question	Is the wood at the bottom harder than the wood at the top?
What to look at? (dependent variable)	The hardness of the wood
What must be different between the things looked at? (independent variable)	The part of the trunk from which blocks of wood are taken
What must be the same? (variables to be controlled)	The direction of grain in the blocks, the position of the block in relation to the bark and the heart wood, etc.
How will the result be used to answer the question?	The results of the same tests on both blocks must be compared to see if the block from the bottom was harder than the block from the top

In an investigation of this kind the greatest difficulty is in making the observations or comparisons. There are no difficult decisions about the independent variable, since there are really no other possibilities. The variables to be controlled might well be controversial because children may not know whether or not certain features affect the hardness. This did happen, for some children mentioned that the blocks should be the same thickness for the test to be fair. To the teacher this seemed to be a misconception of what was meant by 'hardness' (mistaking it for 'strength') but it was left as a suggested control until they had discussed how the hardness was to be compared.

It was not difficult to find ideas for comparing hardness (Science 5/13's Working with Wood, and Learning in Science 'Materials' card on Tools); the problem lay in choosing the best tests for the purpose. The teacher suggested that the children should try out some ideas on some other pieces of wood while they were waiting for the workmen to have time to saw off their samples. They tried a hammer and nail test, but found that the result depended on who was wielding the hammer, so this wasn't good enough. They finally ended up with a contraption to release a sharpened dart from somewhere near the ceiling to fall on to the block on the floor. Positioning the block correctly presented a challenge, solved eventually by a plumbline (and leading to a considerable interest in how vertical some supposedly vertical surfaces in the room were). The safety factor was cared for by erecting a corrugated cardboard screen round the block. It was agreed that the depth of penetration of the dart point would be a measure of the hardness of the wood. During this trial of the measuring procedure, the children who said that the thickness of the blocks should be the same realized that this would not matter, but added 'It will if it makes one higher than the other because the dart won't fall so far'.

So by far the greatest time in the planning (and performance) of this investigation was spent on defining what to compare or measure and how to carry it out in practice. This planning itself involved practical investigation, as we have seen, but it resulted in a very satisfying test of the original question. Without the careful planning it is quite likely that the blocks from the tree would have been subjected to many inconclusive tests and that motivation would have diminished so that little was learned either from the failures or the successes.

Certainly in this case careful planning paid off. But not without some 'trying out'. In this case the general plan was straightforward and the specific plan needed more working out both in thought and action. This is not so in all problems and it is often necessary to make a start with an initial plan and modify it along the way. What determines the feasibility of planning beforehand seems to be the complexity of the necessary procedures in relation to the children's ability to 'think them through'. Very young children are not able to think through an action, unless it is one they are familiar with; they have to *do* and their action and thought go along together. Older children have a greater capacity for thinking through simple actions but still have to 'try and see' when faced with unfamiliar or complex sets of actions.

Children's limited experience means that there must be an interweaving of planning and doing. Nothing said here should be taken as a suggestion that children should be kept from starting an investigation until they have produced a plan acceptable to the teacher. But they will learn a great deal about planning by trying to plan and finding out the limitations of their first attempts by putting them into practice. Gradually they will be able to do more preparation by thinking about the consequence of actions so that not all learning is through making mistakes.

The case for better planning

Although the benefits for children's science education of using and developing planning skills are implicit in much of what has been said already, these probably need to be underlined. It is an unfortunate fact that many teachers place a low priority on this aspect of children's development. This has been a consistent finding of the APU science surveys carried out in England, Wales and Northern Ireland. A questionnaire completed by each school in the surveys (DES 1981) asked teachers to select the five goals they considered the most important from the following:

1 Understanding of basic science concepts.
2 Problem-solving skills.
3 Ability to carry out simple experiments carefully and safely.
4 Enjoyment of science-based work.
5 Knowledge of the natural and physical world around.
6 Ability to observe carefully.
7 Ability to plan experiments.
8 A questioning attitude toward the surroundings.
9 Ability to find information from reference books.
10 Appreciation of relevance of mathematics to real problems.
11 Familiarity with correct use of simple science equipment.
12 Recognition of patterns in observations or data.

The goals consistently rated most highly, across different survey samples and types of school, were numbers 4, 6 and 8. The goal standing out as the lowest priority of all was 7. This result was mirrored in the responses to another question where the teachers were asked to indicate where most emphasis was placed in the science-based activities of the children. Top of the poll was 'make careful observations at first-hand' and bottom, of a list of 18, was 'incorporate controls in experiments'. Since Galton and Simon (1980) concluded from their classroom studies, combined with pupil testing, that pupils' performance reflects their teachers' emphasis on various kinds of classroom experience, it is hardly surprising that the APU survey results show low levels of performance in the planning of investigations.

Evidence of the total absence of experience in planning for the great majority of children was evident in the findings of the survey of primary schools carried out by HM Inspectors in the late 1970s (DES 1978). They found that in less than one class in thirty was there evidence of investigations suggested and planned by the children. The later APU survey results strongly suggest that this may well be because the process of planning is under-valued by teachers. So, before proposing some ways of helping this development, we consider some good reasons for doing so.

The value of planning

Planning helps children in the process of obtaining information from the objects around them

Both the skills of planning and certain attitudes are involved here. The realization that information can be obtained by 'asking the object' (see Chapter 2) leads to a readiness to seek evidence in this way, to find out about things by investigating, observing and getting to know them. The satisfaction of discovery and having one's curiosity satisfied by what has been found fosters a positive attitude to enquiry. This depends upon developing the necessary planning skills so that investigations are carried out in a way that leads to satisfying and unambiguous results.

Planning helps children's approach to problems generally

Planning requires children to think through possible actions. This ability may be limited by general cognitive development, but it is very likely that for many children the absence of experience is a greater limitation. Encouragement to carry out actions in thought should keep pace with maturation so that children become used to using their imagination in this way. Eventually they will be able to think through alternative approaches to a problem and then to pick the one most likely to lead to an unambiguous result.

Planning helps children to rethink ideas

Children's ideas about the world around them are not formed solely on the basis of evidence; more often they are influenced by hearsay and 'everyday', non-scientific, opinion. The *Learning in Science* project findings (see Chapter 7) show clearly that because children have not been taught about such things as force, temperature and characteristics of living things, this does *not* mean that they have no ideas about them. Children pick up ideas in a variety of ways: from parents, peers, the media. These ideas are often in conflict with evidence. For example, many adults believe it to be true that, as stated in one newspaper, 'On a cold night the petrol-station attendant has to handle metal pump controls which are several degrees below the air temperature.' This statement is open to disproof by a very simple investigation such as young children could plan and carry out.

The process of challenging existing ideas should be a fundamental part of science education. Some ideas for helping the rethinking are given in Chapter 7; here we focus upon the role of planning in this process. Planning requires the identification of the evidence that will decide an issue or solve a problem. Often this draws attention to the fact that this evidence has previously never been sought, or has been ignored. It is a simple matter to gather the evidence as to whether a metal which feels colder than its surroundings actually is colder; it is not the difficulty of carrying out the investigation which leaves this fact unchecked, but the willingness to challenge it and think out what evidence is needed to test it in a fair manner.

Similarly, on the same theme, many adults as well as children believe that expanded polystyrene heats up the hand that touches it. This is how some children who investigated the effect of sheets of polystyrene foam came to realise the property of this material that leads to it being described as an insulator. As well as sheets of polystyrene they also had a large cube of the material:

'We were puzzled in our group because the polystyrene feels

warm to your hand. I'm sure I felt warmth when I held the palm of my hand about half an inch away from the cube surface. We thought at first the warmth must come from inside the polystyrene so we drilled a deep hole in one cube, and placed a centigrade thermometer outside near it. But they both said 21 and a half degrees C, so there couldn't be warmth coming from the material. For a long time we were puzzled and couldn't solve the mystery – where was the warmth coming from? Then Penny tumbled on the truth (we think!). The warmth coming from your hand hits the face of the cube and bounces back to your hand. So the material doesn't contain heat, doesn't soak up or absorb the heat – it throws it back. Our teacher says the name for such a material is an insulator . . .'

(DES, 1967, page 245)

A physicist would say that this view of an insulator leaves much to be desired, but for these children it was consistent with their evidence and their reasoning. It was certainly an advance upon the acceptance that the polystyrene cube is producing heat because it feels warm.

Finally the process of planning helps also in clarifying concepts which have to be applied in gathering evidence. An example of this has already been cited in the investigation of the bob-toy (Fig. 6.1), where the concept of rate of motion has to be sorted out from that of duration of motion. The planning and discussion will help some children reject the measurement of duration instead of rate of bobbing; others will realize it only after obtaining a number of results which don't seem to make sense. In both cases the child who has thought out what to measure and carries the plan through is in a better position to rethink ideas than the child who measures the first thing that comes to his mind. Planning helps the children to link up what may otherwise remain as separate parts of their thinking.

Ways of helping children's planning

If one thing is certain, it is that if planning skills are to be developed, then planning must be experienced by carrying it out. The benefits outlined above will not follow if planning is a matter of agreeing with someone else's plan or watching a teacher do the planning. There are three main ways in which teachers can provide children with the experience of planning:

1 By providing opportunities for groups of children to produce plans.

2 By giving children a structure to guide their planning.
3 By discussing, after an investigation, not just the results, but the original plan and how it could now be improved.

Providing opportunities

Children's diet of science-based activities should be a varied and balanced one. It is not necessary or even desirable for the children to propose and plan every investigation for themselves. As the HMI survey suggested, 'The discriminating use of carefully chosen textbooks or assignment cards can help to sustain work in science if their use is carefully planned to supplement a programme of work' (DES, 1978, page 59). However, if working from books or workcards is the only or the main item on the menu, the children will certainly be starved of opportunity for planning. Most workcards, though not all, effectively prevent children from planning by providing a set of instructions to follow.

There will be times when a problem, originating from teacher or pupil, is discussed by the whole class. When various ideas are offered as solutions, the teacher should challenge the children to find out whether their idea is correct or not. Before embarking on an investigation, the children should be set to work out a plan in groups, the task being to agree within the group the actions to be taken. For example, one such occasion followed the replenishing of the water in the aquarium kept in one class. The cloudy water was being syphoned off. It was a slow process and the question was posed as to how it could be speeded up. The teacher asked for ideas as to what might make the water flow out more quickly. Tipping the tank, pressing on the surface of the water, using a wider tube, a longer tube, a shorter tube, putting the end of the tube lower in the water, were all suggested. (There were enough ideas in this case for each group to be working on a different one – though there is no reason why this should always be so.) Before any investigation was started each group presented its ideas to the others. Critical faculties applied to others' plans had probably been sharpened by working on their own plan and they were quick to pounce on points of practicality ('how are you going to press on the water all the way across, then?') or variables not separated ('if you want the tube lower in the tank, you'll need a longer tube and it might be that that makes the difference'). It was a wise move on the part of the teacher to insist on thrashing out plans before carrying out these investigations, where try-and-see methods would have resulted in an even damper classroom floor!

Giving a structure

The understanding of what planning means will develop gradually; it becomes a more elaborate activity as experience increases. But at any point in the course of this development the teacher and the children should have a clear idea of what they should be thinking about and aiming to produce through their planning. The planning steps suggested earlier should be seen as something to aim at; progress will begin for the young and inexperienced children by taking less elaborate steps.

The most helpful way of giving a structure to children's planning is through the idea of the 'fair test'. This can be treated at a range of levels. Infants of 6 and 7 are able to discuss the 'fairness' of a simple test after they have done it; then they gradually become able to think about fairness before doing a test. Taking the idea of fairness further by discussing variables depends upon repeated experience of investigations and should not be hurried. Thinking about what might vary can only fruitfully be done after observing what can vary in a variety of situations. When this transition is made, the structure for thinking about variables can be given in several ways. Here is a very useful suggestion from the Science 5–13 unit *Working with Wood*.

'After discussion they might write, on separate cards, each of the things they decide could vary in their investigation. From their collection of cards they could then select the variable they are investigating ... and line up beside it all the other cards that represent variables that they must try to keep constant...'

The further extension proposed is making an experiment planning board as shown in Fig. 6.2.

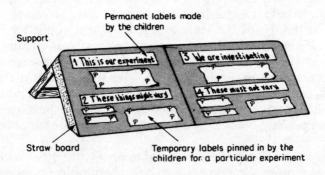

Fig. 6.2

'A planning board can make an exciting contribution to class work, so long as it is introduced when the need arises – when children, through discussion, begin to see the advantage of formalizing their thoughts. If it is introduced too soon or out of context with their immediate work, it is likely to impose a rigidity which defeats the whole point of helping them to develop their ideas'.

(Science 5–13, *Working with Wood*, p. 19)

Discussing possible improvements

Children often indicate dissatisfaction with their investigations in terms of the results. When results are inconclusive, or not what was expected, they describe their experiment as 'no good'. Repeated experience of 'rotten' activities can reduce motivation, but discussion of them can have the double benefit of sharpening self-criticism and reducing the likelihood of the same unfruitful approach being used again. The value of discussion cannot be overemphasized, for planning on its own may otherwise be no more than writing a workcard and then following it.

The principal aim of discussing experiments after they have been done is to develop the habit of self-criticism and reflection on the procedures used. Children require help with this and the teacher should vary the degree of support as the children gradually become able to take over the process themselves. As a start, it may be best to talk with children in groups when their investigation has been finished but before the equipment has been put away. The teacher's questions should be open ones, with no critical implication. 'How did you decide which masses to add to the truck?' 'What results did you get with each one?' 'How did you use the results to decide whether the mass added to the truck made any difference?' Often these kinds of questions are enough to help the children to realize the alternatives that were open to them and the improvements which could have been made. If not, then leading questions help to focus on alternative courses of action. 'Do you think that you'd find the same results if you added a really big mass to the truck?' The discussion should lead the *children* to identify the weaknesses in what they did. The teacher's opinion, if offered, should be part of the general pooling of ideas, not a judgement on the success of the work.

When the children become used to reviewing their work, they will not require someone else to help them reflect on what they did, but will do so spontaneously. Then they can respond to a question such as, 'How would you change the investigation to improve it if you were starting again?' The implication that it can be improved will not be seen as a discouragement when children have reached the point of being self-critical and accepting that there are always different ways of tackling problems and the best way cannot always be foreseen. At this point, too, it is helpful to others to have occasional reporting sessions to the class, where critical comments are invited as each group describes what has been done and found. It is important to see this process as a development and to provide appropriate help for children at different points of it.

Summary of main points

This chapter has included reference to evidence that planning is not being included in children's experience to any extent. Planning skills are important so that children can extend their encounter with the things around them to gather information and ideas in a systematic and satisfying way. Problem-solving ability will improve, too, when children are encouraged to think things out and anticipate useful approaches. Most of all, however, planning skills give children the power to put their own and others' ideas to the test in a scientific way; so they play a central role in developing concepts.

The nature of planning skills has been described and illustrated by examples. It has been suggested that two 'levels' in planning should be distinguished: the general and the specific. At the general level, the variables have to be identified as those which are to be changed or manipulated (the independent variable), those to be observed or measured (the dependent variable) and those to be kept the same for a fair test. At the specific level, the planning concerns the range over which the independent variable is to be changed, how the measurements or observations are to be made and the practical steps to be taken to ensure that other variables are controlled. The development of children's ability to do these things requires teachers to create appropriate opportunities which are summarized in the following guidelines.

Guidelines for helping children to develop planning skills

1 Keep in mind that children don't learn to plan by being told about planning or following plans devised by others; they must plan for themselves.

2 Look carefully and critically at any worksheets or cards that children use. If these do all the planning for the children, don't use them too often; they prevent children from developing planning skills.

3 Start encouraging children to plan with a fairly simple problem (some suggestions follow), chosen so that you know that they will be able to think through what might be done from their experience.

4 Provide a structure to help them think about the 'things' (variables) to be kept the same, or to be changed, and those to be observed or measured.

5 Organize children to prepare plans in groups so that they combine their thinking.

6 Sometimes discuss plans before the children try them in practice and pool ideas for improving the plans.

7 Always review what was planned after the activity so that experience can be used to improve subsequent planning.

8 Some ideas for starting points for taking children through the steps of planning:

(a) Does hot water freeze more quickly than cold water?

(b) Do road signs show up better if the letters are white on black or black on white?

(c) Do tea cosies really keep teapots warm?

(d) Which kind of surface is best for a kitchen worktop?

(e) Is a plastic carrier bag stronger than a paper one?

(f) Does a crushed ice cube melt more quickly or more slowly than a whole one?

(g) Does a soaked bean seed germinate more quickly than one planted without soaking?

7 Children's own concepts

Roger Osborne

Introduction

I recently spent the day with a class of nine-year-old children and their teacher. During the course of the day the children had a lesson on foods and taste. The teacher was well prepared in that she had undertaken some background reading on the subject and had prepared an activity which would involve children tasting various foods. To begin the lesson the teacher asked the class, 'Why do we eat food?' Thirty eager hands leapt skywards. Answers seriously offered included, 'to help us come alive in the morning (breakfast)', 'to stop us feeling hungry', 'so that we don't get tired'. It soon became apparent that while these ideas were listened to by the teacher, they were not the one or ones that she wanted. Each answer in turn received a cursory nod of acceptance from the teacher but was passed over apparently in search of an answer which the teacher considered to be more scientifically acceptable.

We often pay lip service at least to the idea that before we teach a topic it is desirable to first find out what children already know about that topic. Many lessons begin with a question such as 'Why do we eat food?'. Sometimes we may even pre-test children to find out what they already know. And yet, even if we do this, it normally is simply to find out the 'correct' ideas the children have already acquired. How often in a science lesson are we really interested in the non-acceptable (that is, unscientific) ideas that children hold? We so often ignore, in the politest possible way, all the ideas children have which impinge on the topic being taught, or the questions being asked, but which we deem to be not scientifically acceptable.

What are these non-scientific ideas? Are they important in

terms of children's classroom learning? Can we afford to ignore them when we plan what we are going to teach and when we interact with children in the teaching–learning process?

Children's own ideas

Particularly over the last few years, considerable in-depth interview work has been undertaken in various countries to explore children's meanings for words used in science and to determine children's views of the natural and technological world. This work has set out not to establish whether or not children hold acceptable scientific ideas, but to find out the ideas that children hold whatever these meanings and views might be. The work has yielded a wealth of information and has been followed up in certain cases with surveys to ascertain the prevalence of particular viewpoints across representative samples of children at various age levels. All this information, along with interactive observational work in the classroom, has led to the following conclusions:

1 Children have views about a variety of topics in science from a young age, and prior to learning science at school.
2 Children's views are often different from scientists' views, but to children they are sensible, useful views.
3 Children's views can remain uninfluenced, or be influenced in unanticipated ways, by science teaching.

We shall now look at two specific examples to illustrate these points.

Animal

An investigation of children's meanings for the word 'animal' has been carried out by Beverley Bell (Bell, 1981). She showed children pictures of various living things including a cow, a person, a whale, a spider and a worm. For each picture the child was asked, 'In your meaning of the word animal, do you consider this to be an animal?' Irrespective of whether or not the child said yes or no, he or she was asked to give the reasoning which had led to the response. 'Why do you think that?' 'Can you tell me your reasons?' were typical questions asked by the interviewer. Interviews of some of the children surveyed established that many children consider animals to be only the larger land mammals, such as those found on a farm, in a zoo or jungle, or in the home as pets. The reasons used by many children to categorize something as an animal included number of legs (animals have four), size (they are big), habitat (they live on land) and skin covering (animals have fur). Surveys were designed to establish what percentage of children at various age levels consider a cow, a person, a whale, a spider and a worm to be an animal. Typical results are provided in Fig. 7.1. The 16- and 17-year-old pupils were studying biology, all other pupils were studying science.

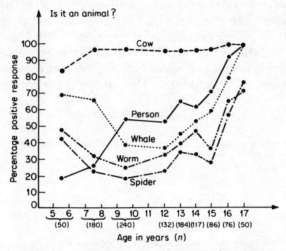

Fig. 7.1 *Survey responses to 'Is it an animal?' (after Bell, 1981)*

The results show that children have ideas about what 'animal' means when they enter school. In some ways the ideas of these young pupils appear more scientifically acceptable than the views held by 12-year-old pupils! The common use of the word animal in statements like 'No animals allowed', 'Animals go to vets while humans go to doctors', 'Animals put humans to shame' (newspaper heading) all reinforce a narrow meaning of the word animal. Teaching which emphasizes sub-categories such as mammals, insects and arachnids may also tend to encourage a restricted use of the word animal. For whatever reason, it would appear that pupils enter secondary school with a limited concept of animal from a biological point of view.

More recent work by Bell and Barker (1982), has shown what happens when secondary teachers attempt to build further learning on a mistaken assumption that 13 year olds have a biologically correct meaning for the word animal. For example it is not helpful if the teacher defines 'consumers' using the statement 'animals are called consumers'!

Electric Current

Children's ideas about electric current in a simple battery–bulb circuit have been investigated in a number of countries (for example, Osborne, 1983). Work which involved interviewing children in the UK, US and New Zealand has suggested that even primary* school children have ideas about how electric current flows in a simple circuit. Four different views about electric current in a simple circuit have been found to be held by children. These four views are described in Fig. 7.2. The majority of primary children given a battery, bulb and wires attempt to light the bulb by connecting the top terminal of the battery to the base of the bulb. Even when these children are shown that a second wire is necessary, some of them still retain, what we call a Model A view of current flow: 'The current goes from the battery

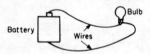

A battery is connected up to a torch bulb as shown in the diagram. The bulb is glowing

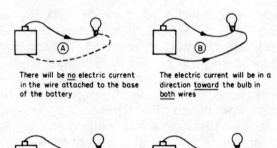

In the way you think about it, the <u>electric current</u> in the wires is best described by which diagram ?

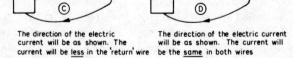

There will be <u>no</u> electric current in the wire attached to the base of the battery

The electric current will be in a direction <u>toward</u> the bulb in <u>both</u> wires

The direction of the electric current will be as shown. The current will be <u>less</u> in the 'return' wire

The direction of the electric current will be as shown. The current will be <u>same</u> in both wires

Fig. 7.2 *The four common ideas described by children for current flow in a simple battery–bulb circuit (A–D)*

* In the context of this chapter, 'primary' includes children up to the age of 13.

to the bulb where it is all used up.' The non-current carrying wire is sometimes considered by these children to be 'a sort of switch' (initiates current flow) or a kind of safety wire. Model B is a very popular model among primary children: 'The currents clash in the bulb causing it to light up.' Model C is a view held more frequently by older children. These children seem to appreciate the circulatory nature of current but they consider that 'some current must be used up to make the bulb glow'. Finally Model D is the accepted scientific view. While even some nine year olds hold this view, it is not the most popular view. Young children when asked what they think of Model D tend to reject it. 'How could the bulb light or the battery go flat?' they ask.

Using the question in Figure 7.2, some indication of the prevalence of these views at various age levels has been obtained. The results in Fig. 7.3 were obtained in New Zealand. All pupils of 15 years of age or less were studying science; the 16 and 17 year olds were studying physics.

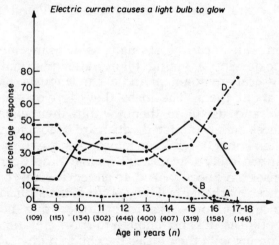

Fig. 7.3 *Survey response to the question shown in Figure 7.2.*

Despite the teaching of simple ideas about electric circuits prior to age 16, the results indicate that a non-scientific viewpoint (Model C) becomes increasingly popular as children get older, and that there is very little change in the percentage of pupils who consider Model D to be the best viewpoint up to age 16. An analysis of the teacher's guide material available to New Zealand teachers on the teaching of simple circuits, suggests that children are assumed to somehow acquire a Model D view of electric current almost immediately they discover that a complete circuit is required for the bulb to light. On the basis of the interviews we have done, we would be surprised if the situation is very different in other countries.

Why are these things happening?

While we have provided only two specific examples of children's ideas and how these ideas differ at different age levels, many other similar examples could be cited. Children's views about *boiling* (what are the large bubbles in boiling water made of?); about *burning* (what are the products of a candle burning?); about *force* (why does a golf ball move through the air in the way that it does?); about *gravity* (is gravity greater or less the higher up you go?); about *friction* (does a person sitting on a slide have any frictional forces acting on him or her?); about *plants* (is a carrot a plant?); about *living* (is a fire living?) and many other topics all yield interesting information about children's ideas and how the prevalence of these views is not always influenced by teaching in the way we might hope (Osborne, Freyberg, 1984). Why are these things happening? Possible reasons include:

1 Children's ideas can be strongly held. Many ideas would appear to develop, as young children attempt to make sense of their physical environment and of the language used by the people about them. The ideas they develop are sensible, plausible and useful to them, within their experience. If experiences are encountered which are in conflict with these ideas, then either the children may appreciate some limitation on the applicability of an idea or they may simply consider that their senses have been tricked. In either case, one or two such experiences, particularly if they occur in the artificial world of the science laboratory or classroom, do not bring about a major rethink of ideas. It is not enough to show children examples which conflict with their ideas; the children must reconstruct their ideas for themselves.

2 Teachers are often unaware of children's non-scientific ideas. This is not surprising. As indicated earlier we are not encouraged to do more than find out the acceptable scientific ideas children already hold. Teacher's guide material rarely, if ever, provides information on those non-scientific children's ideas which nevertheless could influence children's thinking about a particular situation or topic. In the complex world associated with classroom teaching, it is so difficult for a teacher to listen

to, analyse, and record children's ideas at the same time as teaching thirty or more children. (See the Appendix to this chapter on page 87, where there is an account of a formal science lesson which illustrates this only too well and from which points equally applicable to other teaching contexts are drawn.)

3 Teachers often make unfounded assumptions about the teaching and learning process. While it might be appropriate when teaching some topics to assume that children have empty heads waiting to be filled up with knowledge, such an assumption about teaching and learning is clearly inadequate in many science lessons. Even to assume that if children have ideas prior to teaching these will be rapidly lost and replaced by taught ideas, seems to be false in many situations. Children *do have* prior ideas, which *do* have considerable influence on their learning.

4 There is often a severe problem of lack of communication between teacher and pupils. When two people communicate, what passes between them are the words and gestures they use to attempt to convey meaning, not the meaning itself. So a teacher has some ideas which he or she hopes to convey by putting them into words, diagrams or symbols. The child may take note of the words, and so on, but from these has to build up a meaning for them. There is clearly a strong possibility that this meaning created by the child is not the meaning intended by the teacher. This possibility is very high if the type of language used by the teacher, or workcard, or textbook writer, is not familiar to the child. Then various things may happen, as Barnes (1976) has so clearly pointed out:

(a) The child may ignore what the teacher is saying.
(b) The teacher may ignore what the pupil is saying (the teacher 'controls' knowledge by using unfamiliar language, consequently the children's ideas are devalued and are only heard when they talk among themselves).
(c) The teacher may insist that the pupils use the 'correct' words and so sound scientific. (We, like Barnes, have seen children praised for 'thinking like a scientist' when it is clear that the children are simply 'making noises which sound scientific'.)

Why do we want to change children's ideas?

If children have strongly held views about how and why things behave as they do, and the views children hold are intelligible, plausible and useful views to them, then one must ask why do we want to change children's ideas? This brings us to the point of asking what are, or should be, the aims of science teaching?

While there can be many possible answers to this question, it is our view that one of the main aims of science teaching, at any level, is to help people make better sense of their world. Better, in that in acquiring a new perspective on a topic or situation the learner considers it to be more satisfactory, that is, more intelligible, plausible and useful, than his or her earlier ideas.

In addition to this aim, it is our view that as teachers of science we want pupils, particularly as they get older, to recognize many scientific ideas as ones that are useful to society. Further we would like our future technologists and scientists to adopt these accepted scientific ideas as their own. Moreover, we would like them to adopt them because *they*, personally, find them to be intelligible, plausible and useful ideas.

Undoubtedly there will be some readers who will agree with the above but who will state that we should leave pupils to develop their own ideas or that one of our problems is that we force scientific ideas on children at too young an age. While accepting this to some extent, our work suggests to us that if pupils are left to develop their own ideas they will not invariably arrive at good scientific explanations. This may well endanger the value of later learning opportunities for it seems quite possible that patterns of thought can ossify as a pupil gets older.

But there is no reason why children should be left to their own ideas. The role of the teacher in the class is to do more than provide equipment and an organization for children to use it. The teacher can use various strategies to intervene constructively in children's experience and thinking.

What can teachers do?

There are no simple answers to the problem of children's ideas limiting the effectiveness of our teaching. However certain things can be suggested.

We need to accept that children's ideas can have an inordinate influence on the teaching–learning process and to appreciate and be sensitive to, the range of possible outcomes of any teaching–learning interaction. Children do not have blank minds that will easily discard old ways of thinking: ways of thinking which have been used relatively successfully to make sense of the world from a young age. We need to appreciate that direct teaching can have surprisingly little affect on these ideas. Taught ideas can be ignored, misinterpreted or stored in a separate corner of memory, so that a child's way of thinking about how and why things behave as they do is at best unchanged or at worst reinforced by misinterpreted taught knowledge. Alternatively children can become confused or even bemused by the impact of teaching on their earlier ideas. We have interviewed pupils who appear no longer to have any ideas about particular topics that could really be useful to them or anyone else. There are, of course, the success stories, where children develop scientific ideas which are integrated into their way of thinking and which are useful to them; undoubtedly this state of affairs is the one that teachers would like to aim for. However, to be unduly optimistic that this state has been reached in earlier lessons, and to design advanced learning on the possibly false assumption that elementary scientific ideas will necessarily be clearly understood by our pupils, is to build learning on faulty foundations.

If it is accepted that the ideas that children bring to a lesson are of critical importance then we need to be aware of what is already known about children's ideas and about how these ideas can be influenced. There are several groups of researchers working to reveal the nature of children's own ideas relating to scientific concepts. Some examples of their findings are given in Table 7.1.

Unfortunately, less information is available about how to influence children's firmly held ideas. On the basis of what we know already the following suggestions are made:

1 We need to be aware of children's ideas as well as the ideas of scientists about a particular topic.
2 Pupils need to have experience of and be familiar with, the phenomena in which the ideas to be discussed are embedded. Wherever possible this should involve the children in first-hand experience. For example, children need to be very familiar with wiring batteries and bulbs *before* we start discussing ideas about electric current. It is in such practical situations that we need to raise questions in children's minds, to get them to think out answers and encourage them to clarify ideas.
3 If we are to attempt to change children's ideas, we need to encourage children to express their ideas, to present them to others and to appreciate the views of others, including the teacher's view.
4 The value of the modified ideas should be made evident by using them to solve new problems and applying them to make sense of new experience.

The importance of communication, stressed in point 3 but latent in all four points above, cannot be over-emphasized. This is to be valued for the process of a child organizing his or her thoughts as much as for the product in which these thoughts are made available to others. As Barnes (1976) puts it, 'The desire to communicate with others plays a dynamic part in the organization of knowledge ... What is in question is whether schools do in fact challenge pupils to communicate *their* viewpoints so that they are available to other people with different assumptions.'

Thus, through reasoning, experimentation (or the consider-

Table 7.1 *Some of children's own ideas*

Force and motion	Many children consider force to be something which is *in* a body, acting in the direction of motion. A physicist considers a force acts *on* a body causing changes in motion; force can be acting in a direction opposite to that of the motion.
Friction and motion	Many children associate friction only with motion and do not consider frictional forces exist if two surfaces are not moving relative to each other. To a physicist frictional forces can exist in these stationary situations.
Force of gravity	The physicists' view of the earth's force of gravity is that it gradually decreases as the distance above the earth's surface increases and that it is independent of the presence of air. However, to many children gravity is strongly associated with the presence of air, it increases as the distance above the earth's surface increases, but is zero beyond the earth's atmosphere.
Light	To many children, and to scientists, light travels away from a source. However, to children, how far it travels is considered to depend on how far from the source the visible effects of the light can be observed, e.g. does it appear to illuminate a wall? Hence many children consider light from a candle travels only about a foot in daylight but travels further in the dark! To a physicist the light continues in a straight line until it is absorbed or reflected by some object.
Plants	Children tend to restrict their view of plants to things planted in the vegetable or flower garden. They tend to exclude a number of things that biologists would consider to be plants, e.g. mature trees.

These ideas were found by interviewing children as part of the *Learning in Science Project* in New Zealand (Freyberg, Osborne and Tasker, 1983).

ation of observations and experiences) and communication, the child may realize that there are different ideas from his own and come to perceive the scientific viewpoint as more intelligible, plausible and useful than the originally held ideas. In the Appendix on page 87 is a description of a lesson in which many of the features of learning and teaching just mentioned were sadly lacking. Although it concerns a formal science lesson it nonetheless illustrates the challenge faced by all teachers in the knowledge that children's own ideas are important. It has been suggested (Nussbaum and Novick, 1981) that new roles could well be incorporated into a teacher's activity and into his or her self-image. These roles include:

1 *The teacher as physician*. Here we might think of the teacher as diagnosing that children have particular ideas, where such ideas are known to exist, and discovering children's ideas for topics where children's ideas are not known.
2 *The teacher as listener*. To diagnose and discover children's ideas we need to provide opportunities for children to express these in small groups and in the whole class setting. If children are to express their ideas openly we need to provide a classroom climate where such ideas are valued and listened to.
3 *The teacher as inventor*. Possibly the most difficult task of all, once children's ideas are known, is to be innovative and to invent new ways to help children perceive scientific ideas as more intelligible, plausible and useful than the ones they hold at present.
4 *The teacher as experimenter*. It is important that we evaluate, as objectively as possible, new insights into children's ideas and new ways of modifying children's ideas.
5 *The teacher as researcher*. Good experimentation involves sharing findings about children's ideas and sharing successes and failures about children's ideas with other teachers.

The findings about children's ideas also raise questions about the aims of science teaching, including how and at what age a child should be introduced to an acceptable scientific viewpoint; where this is different from the child's own view of a particular situation or topic. While there has been much discussion in recent years about the inadvisability of introducing scientific ideas at too young an age, it is possible that older children can develop such a complex and inflexible framework of ideas that further learning becomes increasingly difficult. While there are no simple solutions to these problems, we need to base our teaching on realistic assumptions about the teaching–learning process and build on our limited knowledge of children's ideas.

Summary of main points

Children come to science activities with their own ideas about the things that are studied, rather than with empty spaces in their minds ready to be filled with new ideas. Their existing ideas are likely to be rather different from the accepted 'scientific' ones and will strongly influence the sense children make of the activities they undertake. Unless teachers take particular care to find out about children's existing ideas and take deliberate steps to help children rethink their ideas and try out new ones as well as their own, these non-scientific ideas tend to persist and keep out the accepted scientific ones.

The above are some of the findings from research carried out by interviewing children about their ideas on a variety of scientific concepts. The examples described in this chapter are about children's ideas of 'animal' and 'electric current'; findings about other concepts have been mentioned in brief. The possible reasons for the state of affairs revealed by this and other similar research have been discussed. They include the cumulative effect of teachers ignoring children's own ideas, and the problem of communication, when teachers use words in their scientific meaning and pupils take them as having a different, often 'everyday' meaning. Some reasons for wanting to change children's ideas have been proposed and the suggestions made for ways of bringing about change can be summarized as follows.

Guidelines for changing children's ideas

1 Find out what ideas children already have about a phenomenon or situation; what do they think is happening, for what reasons, what words do they use to explain or describe it?
2 Take children's ideas seriously; give them the opportunity to try out their ideas by investigating the objects or situations for themselves.
3 Challenge children in discussion to find evidence for their own ideas.
4 Organize whole-class discussions so that different ideas about the same things can be brought together.
5 Enable children to become aware of ideas different from their own and to try them out.
6 Offer them a scientific view as one worth trying as well as

others; don't insist that it is 'right' but let children explore its value for themselves.

7 Provide challenges for them to use new or modified ideas in trying to solve other problems or to make sense of new experience.

Appendix to Chapter 7

To illustrate the kind of evidence which has uncovered the issues discussed in Chapter 7 we give an example of a lesson involving 12 year olds (Tasker, 1982). It is teacher-directed, but activity-based. The class is taught as a whole, but the problems the teacher encounters might be equally prevalent in dealing with groups on the same or different activities.

In this lesson pupils had the experience of heating water in a flask and observing the water turn to steam, recondense in a tube connected to the flask and drip into a beaker. The teacher hoped that through this experience children would develop ideas about the change of state of water in terms of the particle model. In the class discussion at the end of the activity, pupils commented that when the water was heated gas went up the tube. The teacher then stated

'Right, correct . . .OK. That tube is fairly cold on the outside, once the water vapour hits the side of the tube . . . it recondenses into water which comes out the end.'

At this point in the lesson the teacher used volunteer pupils to model evaporation. Five pupils were asked to stand in a line at the front of the class with their adjacent feet touching and with the middle pupil holding the nearest hand of the pupils on each side. The pupils were instructed to wriggle vigorously while the teacher talked.

Teacher: Right, stand in a line and jostle . . . as the water heats more and more they start wriggling and moving a lot faster . . . so people in the middle . . . middle three start wriggling as fast as you can . . . what's going to happen to the people at the ends? (no one answers and nothing happens). Come on you people start really moving.

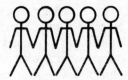

Fig. App. 7.1

Paul: They smack off.

Teacher: (ignores comment) You are not meant to be moving ...
           just stand still at the ends ... come on good shoves
           from the middle as you are getting hotter and hotter.

           (one end pupil stumbles away)

           Right ... OK. One end's fallen off ... and that's what
           happens to the particles in the liquid ... sit down you
           didn't really do that very well ... Right, as heat is
           applied the particles start wriggling and jiggling
           around ... and they jiggle the top particles of the
           liquid up in the form of a gas and it goes up the tube ...
           it recondenses and then it comes out the end.

           (The class were then given the following instructions)

           Write your observations and explain them by talking
           about particles ... I want you to explain what
           happened inside the water in terms of particles as heat
           was applied ... I expect to see diagrams explaining
           and showing particles and what happens.

That the experience had significance relating to particle
behaviour was clear in the mind of the teacher – what were the
pupils saying and doing?

George: What do we do?

Judy: How do you spell 'gauze' ... here it is (finds word in a
           diagram of an earlier investigation) G ... A ... U ... Z
           ... E.

Jenny: Equipment is on the board.

Judy: I know.

George: I missed out gauze, burner and tripod ... how do you
           spell gauze?

Judy: G ... A ... U ... Z ... E

Jenny: Look at the board.

Paul: That there is called tripod, that there is gauze, that's
           the ...

Judy: Burner.

George: No, that's the burner ... that's the glass (burner
           cover).

Teacher: (interrupting) I've written a few words on the board
           that might help you with your write-up ... evapor-
           ates, recondenses and vigorous ... particles move in a
           vigorous fashion so that they were able to lift off the
           top of the solution.

Paul: That glass thing that you put on . . .
Jenny: It's a rubber stopper.
Paul: (writes label) Rubber stopper.

At this point Jenny, who was ahead of the others, wrote the subheading 'Conclusion' in her book and after it, 'We found that when we put the water on the burner it made air bubbles'. When Jenny was not looking George and Judy copied Jenny's statement into their own books which they then closed quickly before Jenny noticed.

How had the experiences of observation and class discussion influenced children's ideas about the basic phenomena and events involved in the lesson? The extract below is part of a conversation similar to a number held with individual pupils after the lesson.

Paul: When water is boiled it evaporates – turns into gases and goes off from there and turns into air.
Judy: The heat is sort of like . . . pushing out all these little . . . mmm gas . . .
Observer: The gas is in the water?
Paul: I think they are in the water – when it gets heated . . . they come out.
Observer: The gas . . . has that anything to do with water or what?
Paul: It's in the water.
Observer: It's not water?
Paul: No.

At the end of the lesson the observer talked to the teacher, who revealed some dissatisfaction with aspects of the lesson and the unit of work. However these stated dissatisfactions related to equipment and managerial aspects of handling groups of children. Only one comment was made about the scientific ideas that the children might have developed during the lesson.

Teacher: I think the concepts are getting a bit thrashed . . . but actually it's all right – I think they are understanding it, but I think the interest isn't there as much as it was.

To the observer, this comment confirmed that the teacher had no real appreciation of children's ideas. There was no appreciation of the lack of impact, of much of what had been presented, on the children's ideas about changes of state of water.

While the number of problems and difficulties with this particular lesson may be atypically large, they reflect in nature the sorts of problems found in many classrooms and discussed in general terms on pages 80–82.

Communication

As far as we were able to detect, ideas of 'particles', 'moving in a vigorous manner', 'evaporates' and 'recondenses', had no impact whatever on the children we observed in the lesson. In fact teacher and pupils appeared to be in two different worlds: the teacher in the world of theory, the pupils in the world of reality. This is something we have observed in a number of classrooms. The children's ideas were only heard in their talk with each other about the burner, the gauze and the rubber stopper. These details seemed to assume more importance than the phenomenon they were observing. Perhaps the lack of encouragement to express in their own words ideas about 'the steam' or 'the water disappearing and reappearing' provided little opportunity to focus their thinking on, or have their thinking challenged with respect to, those things which the teacher considered central to the lesson.

The purpose of the lesson

The original purpose of the lesson intended by the teacher was for children to investigate the expansion of a liquid. This was made explicit on the blackboard (see Fig. App. 7.2)

Expansion of a liquid

Method: Fill a flask with coloured water.
Mark the level of the water in the tube.
Heat the flask using a burner.

Observe what happens to the water level.

Explain why this happens by talking about particles.

Fig. App. 7.2

The apparatus supplied to the children had stoppers with a short length of tubing attached to a length of clear plastic tubing. The children found it extremely difficult to fit the stoppers into full flasks of water. However, they overcame this problem by emptying out some of the water. The purpose to the children then became heating the water, observing the boiling, watching the recondensed water dripping from the plastic tube. As we have seen the teacher changed the 'purpose' of the activity to follow the direction taken by the pupils. This of course does not necessarily happen. In many classrooms only some pupils construct a purpose which is obviously different from that intended. Sometimes, even frequently, pupils construct a purpose subtly different to that intended by the teacher.

One consequence of pupils not appreciating the teacher's intended purpose for a teacher directed activity, or pupils constructing even a subtly different purpose to the one constructed by the teacher, is that the critical design features of the activity may not be appreciated. In the above example, the critical necessity to have the tube immersed in the liquid was not appreciated by pupils, nor pointed out or explained to them.

The significant results

The pupils did not appear to share the teacher's view about what were the significant results of the activity. The pupils focused on the concrete aspects of the activity. What concerned the teacher, the changes of state of water in the adapted experiment, were not really the focus of pupil attention nor seen by pupils as providing interesting and significant results.

The children's ideas

The children's ideas remained basically unaffected by the alternative views presented by the teacher. the teacher's views were presented in a way which tended to make them either not particularly intelligible, plausible or useful, or led pupils to constructions which were not intended. The children's idea that 'the gas in the water comes out when the water is heated' was not challenged. In fact when the interviewer discussed a child's idea at the end of the lesson, the pupil's original ideas appear to have been reinforced. Presumably to Paul his ideas about the bubbles were not only intelligible and plausible to him but also useful in that they 'explained' the observations. Moreover if Paul thought the 'particles in the liquid' which the teacher talked about were the bubbles, then the teacher's statement like 'they jiggle the top particles off in the form of a gas', simply reinforces his view. While the teacher had appreciated that the pupils had constructed a purpose and an activity different to that intended, it would appear that the teacher had not really appreciated the lack of impact of this lesson on the way many of the pupils in the class viewed the changes of state of water.

8 Children communicate

Jos Elstgeest, Wynne Harlen and David Symington

It could be said that a good question is more important than its answer; a well-defined problem invites sound scientific activity in order to find a good answer. A good question is the first scientific step towards its answer. This applies in the laboratory, in research and no less in the classroom. Further, good questions lead to communication between the teacher and the children, or among the children themselves. Communication is a vital aspect of the progress of science. It can take various shapes, but it never takes the shape of a teacher dictating summaries, nor of a child chanting memorized answers. In this chapter we consider communication involving children and science of three kinds: various types of discussion; notebooks or folders; drawing, painting and modelling.

Discussion

Whole-class discussion

First of all there is the free and open communication of the class discussion; 'class conversation' is a better phrase. This often takes place after some work has been accomplished and before activities are resumed, or new ones initiated. A good time for these talks seems to be at the beginning of a lesson period for, once the children are off on to new explorations, it might be difficult to bring them together, or to catch their attention. It is best to try not to interrupt them at awkward moments, just when something begins to happen. But sound judgement is needed, for when work threatens to develop in a wrong direction, one has to interfere. The teacher can often make arrangements beforehand to stop working at a certain time in order to compare notes and to report to each other. The children will then know what to expect.

A class conversation is a form of communication where the most generous sharing of ideas is made possible. It frequently kindles new interests, invites the testing of new ideas which the children put forward, challenges others' work, proposes possible answers to remaining problems, or opens up new lanes of discovery and exploration. The teacher's contribution is as much part of the conversation as any of the children's and if it is accepted it is not because of authority, but through the power of conviction. This gives the teacher a chance to make unobtrusive corrections, to give further encouragement, to point out relationships, to highlight what is relevant and to obscure what is trivial. The children's own contributions are often of great impact; they challenge each other more effectively than the teacher by insisting on clarity of explanation, or by comparing results of similar, or repeated, experiments. Children correct each other by conviction, not through obedience.

This positive, helping atmosphere will not be created without some structure. People have to listen in conversations, as well as speak and it is up to the teacher to manage the exchange so that those taking part have equal say and equal chance both to ask and to answer questions. This role in relation to the *structure* of the discussion does not mean that the teacher dominates or determines the *content* of the exchanges. Acting rather like a chairman, the role is to help the discussion keep to one subject until everyone has said what they have to say about it. This will often mean delaying some comments brought up on a different topic and the teacher must remember to return to them at a later point.

It is also worth arranging the class in a way that fosters participation in the discussion. Depending on the size of the children and of the room, it may be helpful to bring the children to one part of the class, perhaps sitting on the floor, as they might do when listening to a story. This focuses attention on the shared topic and encourages children to take part and throw some ideas into the exchange. It is difficult for some children to muster the courage to speak if they are physically separated from the teacher by what seems to them an enormous distance.

Small-group discussion with the teacher

We shall now look at the communication between the teacher and the working group, or the invidual. Children usually delight in showing or describing what they are doing or what they have discovered or accomplished. They chat incessantly among themselves, or to nobody in particular, but they easily make the teacher a partner of the conversation, provided they have something about which to communicate and provided they are ready to communicate with their teacher. If they are not, then they are better left alone for a while.

Anna was a rather shy little girl. She was not yet very confident in herself. She was working with a ruler. Something was going on. The teacher happened to pass her and, in his eagerness, wanted her to talk about her work.

'What are you doing, Anna?' he asked.

Anna did not reply. She started fiddling with her ruler and stopped whatever she was doing. The interruption was just too much for her at this stage of her work. But this teacher would not give up and insisted: 'Are you measuring something?'

'Yes', whispered Anna.

'What are you measuring?'

'... ??? ... giggle ... ???'

'Are you measuring your desk or your book?'

'Yes.'

This conversation makes it plain that, if the teacher had asked Anna 'Are you measuring the moon?', she would have promptly whispered 'Yes.' The odds are that Anna was not measuring anything at all! Why didn't the teacher leave Anna alone? The conversation did not make him any wiser, and it put Anna completely off whatever she was doing. Eventually she would have shown signs of wanting to share her work with somebody, perhaps by showing it to a friend, or, perhaps, by drawing a picture or writing something in her workbook.

Small-group discussion without the teacher

There is also discussion among members of a working group when the teacher is not present. This is probably the most important kind of discussion of all, for here children are free to exchange, with equals, even the most seemingly far-fetched or half-formed ideas. And by listening to others' ideas, they realize that there are different ways of thinking about and explaining things. They will argue and challenge others' views and have to defend their own. Eventually they may as a group come to a position or hold a view different from the starting point of any of them. Their combined thinking has produced something better than any individual's thinking. They will have learned that an

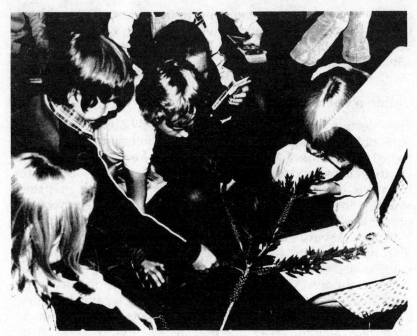

Fig. 8.1

idea is no use unless there is evidence for it. The kind of evidence that is needed to stand up to the logical prodding of their peers also becomes apparent to each one.

A great deal has already been said in earlier chapters about the value of discussion in fostering the development of particular skills and ideas. Much of what has been said draws upon or refers to the work of Douglas Barnes (1976), who argued eloquently that children's thinking and talking are intimately connected. Consequently, the more children can 'think aloud' in informal discussions, the more they can take the responsibility for formulating their own ideas. When the teacher is not present they cannot depend upon the 'right' answer being supplied (if they will only wait long enough), they have to struggle to find their own solutions.

Many teachers worry that when children are working in groups, they cannot adequately supervise all the groups at once. If they can only be one place at a time, how can the other groups be taught? The answer is that the other groups will be learning in a way that they *cannot* do if the teacher is with them and that this is a most valuable kind of learning. Indeed it is just as well that the teacher cannot be with every group all the time, otherwise children would not have the opportunity of discussion without the presence of 'an authority'. Absence of this presence frees them, and obliges them, to think aloud and have their thinking criticized by others.

Children's notebooks

This section concerns the use of workbooks, folders or notebooks for children to keep their own notes and make some record of the work. Some of it will be in the form of drawings and painting, discussed further in the next section. Here we focus on the value of using notebooks and ways of encouraging this, avoiding the tedium of 'writing up' which spoils the excitement of science activities for so many children.

Work/notebooks are a very special, but very essential means of communication, too often neglected or underestimated in value. Notebooks used well give not only stability and permanence to children's work, but also purpose and form. They are a record, an extension of their mental activities, a paper memory, a store of personally valued information. Notebooks can contain such unsayable things as drawings, tables or graphs and are an essential item in the children's scientific tool bag. The keeping of records and the organization of data often require paperwork, but on top of that children like it and are proud of something which they can show off. They may start to use notebooks at a very early stage in their scientific career, even before they know how to write. Drawings are a means of self-expression but, even before that, the discovery that pencils make lines, that ink makes blots, that crayons leave coloured tracks and that paints leave lovely smears, is an early form of recording on paper.

As is the case with all other skills and abilities, children need time and plenty of opportunity to practise in order to develop their skill of self-expression, which will gradually improve so as to become real communication. In the earliest stages, children want a notebook to draw what they see and to write or draw about what they think is going on. It may well be that only they, themselves, understand these scribbles and sketches. The drawings may well diverge from reality and be filled with imaginative additions and embellishments; they will be naturally clumsy and childish in comparison with the artistic illustrations in books, but that is how it should be, for the notebooks are the children's own, while the printed books are not.

Later, notebooks become useful instruments for recording

experiments and their results, and the teacher must see to it that the children learn to record what they actually see and do, and not what they think the teacher expects them to have seen or done. Sooner or later the children will have to record data so as to be able to compare results of experiments which require intervals of time. The earlier the children start to learn to keep records, the better they will be prepared to make it an integral part of their science activities. The nature of the notes to be taken depends, of course, on the kind of observation, investigation or experiment being done. Especially at later stages, it will become necessary to note times or distances or data on other measurements, as soon as they are taken or verified, because interpretation of such data requires a running record. Well-trained children will recognize the need for such sustained records themselves.

Using a notebook or making some kind of record should become a normal part of science work; but interrupting a child in the middle of an activity to insist on his writing something will not achieve this end. It is better to wait till he feels satisfied that he has 'done' something, and really has something to write about. Children often want to consult their teacher before they start writing, but not always. It is of the utmost importance for the teacher to realize and to acknowledge that the children's science notebooks are their own workbooks, and not the teacher's trap to test them. This does not mean that the teacher may not look at the books in order to detect the children's progress, we shall deal with that later. But too often the children associate their notebooks with the exercise of 'answering the teacher's questions'.

It happened in a fourth-year class (mainly 10-year-olds). The teacher could no longer resist 'finding out what the children understand'. For two lesson periods he had allowed them to experiment freely with balances. During the third period he wrote questions on the blackboard. There is, of course, nothing against writing suggestive questions on the blackboard, but since the teacher told the children to answer these in their notebooks, they became test questions to the children. One of the questions read, 'If you make one side of the balance heavier than the other, what will the balance look like? Draw a picture.' Since this was a writing exercise, the balances were left untouched in the process.

Louis drew Fig. 8.2 in his notebook.

Because of the question asked the teacher had no alternative: Louis' picture was 'wrong'. A bad mark for Louis. Does this

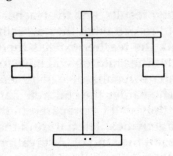

Fig. 8.2

mean, however, that Louis did not understand what happens to a balance when one side is heavier? Talking to Louis for only one minute made it abundantly clear that he perfectly understood what happens to a balance of which one side is made heavier. 'Can you make the right side heavier than the left?' , he was asked. Louis promptly added a weight to the pan on the right, and the arm swung down. 'Can you now make the left side heavier?' Louis removed the weight that he had just put on the right-hand side. The left arm of the balance see-sawed down. Not only did Louis know what happens to the heavier side, he also knew two ways of regulating the weights: add to one side or subtract from the other. Fortunately, because of this little conversation, the teacher got a better impression of Louis' understanding of the working of the balance.

What would the teacher's conclusion have been if he had only looked at Louis' notebook? He would have most probably thought that Louis knew nothing about balances and he would have expressed a low opinion about the work by some mark or remark on Louis' work. Yet Louis knew a great deal more about balances than the blackboard question had asked for. He just did not make a good job of drawing what he knew: his line of communication was blocked. This was not Louis' fault, it was the mistake of the teacher. He should have given Louis a chance to express his own findings in his own way. If the teacher had simply encouraged Louis, and his classmates, to write and draw about his own experiments with the balance, and had spent time in helping him communicate his ideas clearly, then both would have profited more from the exercise. The teacher would have learned more about Louis, and his classmates, and Louis would have learned better how to express himself.

Let us assume that Louis would have drawn his picture in the same way, and had labelled it to indicate that 'the left side is heavier'. No longer restricted by his blackboard question, the teacher can now begin to find out why Louis made the illustration the way he did. Is it because he does not yet grasp the idea of 'heavier' in connection with the behaviour of the balance? Or is it because Louis did not observe the position of the arms of the balance properly? A similar conversation to the one described above would have made it clear that Louis' difficulty does not lie there. But Louis probably had trouble drawing illustrations which accurately represent what he sees. This is not so unusual among young children. There is always a reason why children drawn the conclusions they do and why they communicate their ideas in a certain way. The task of the teacher is not to tell them that their descriptions or illustrations are right or wrong. The task of the teacher is to help the children develop skills of careful observation and of clear self-expression. In this case it would not have been difficult for the teacher, nor for Louis, to consider together, 'Does the drawing really look like the balance with a heavier left side?'

Children use their notebooks to express themselves and to communicate; they are like mirrors. They reflect the child's ideas in many ways and so serve as a guide to the understanding teacher. These notebooks help the teacher to know what the children have thought about, how they have thought about it, what they have observed, what they have or have not understood and, above all, what they have been, or still are, interested in. These notebooks also help the teacher to recognize which children can work independently and imaginatively and which ones would need more encouragement and attention.

Making good use of the children's notebooks for evaluating their progress is very important indeed, but beware of old habits, virtuous as they may seem. No sooner does a teacher get a child's notebook, than out flips the red pencil. Red pencils are manufactured for correcting and marking. But in science education a child uses a notebook to try to express himself, and so to develop his ability to communicate. In other words: a child uses a notebook in order to learn how to use a notebook. Many children, especially those who are just beginning to learn to express themselves in writing, have difficulty in putting their thoughts into words. For a long time most children have difficulty in organizing their thoughts in a logical order. So what good would it do to a child if the teacher were to put a grade or a mark to his attempts to communicate in writing or drawing or sketching? How is a mark, good or bad, going to assist a child in writing his own ideas better next time?

Where a sound relationship has been established, and where

children are relaxed and confident in their work, they talk freely with their teacher, and listen to his contributions with eagerness and confidence. Likewise they become aware that they can communicate with their teacher through their notebook as well. In this relationship the teacher can fruitfully add comments to the children's work and write them in the notebooks. The children will accept this gratefully as a matter of course. The teacher may suggest a new word to use. When a child writes, 'My piece of chalk floats on the water and bubbles come out. Then it goes to the bottom', the teacher may add, 'it sinks'. Or, coming back from a field-trip, a child notes, 'I saw an insect and it pushed a ball of cow droppings'. Here the comment, 'Cow droppings are called 'dung', and the insect is called dungbeetle' would be in place. These sorts of remarks, instead of leaving a bad feeling of failure, give encouragement to the children who often want to know the right word, simply because they are keen to express themselves well and clearly.

Another way of helping children is to make suggestions on how to clarify their thought, or how to organize their notes. Useful little hints, like drawing dividing lines, preparing a table to collect measurements or observations, numbering recordings of separate experiences, or connecting part of a drawing to its label can be given or inserted in their notebooks whenever it seems desirable. Children's understanding can profit from the teacher's helpful remarks in order to improve their skills of recording. Even suggesting a certain pattern as a model for recording will do no harm, provided there remains flexibility and choice enough to fit any circumstance.

It often happens that children's written records are incomplete, their illustrations less accurate than desirable, as in the case of Louis. How does the teacher correct these shortcomings? In a nutshell, the answer is by not correcting anything. Correction is the children's responsibility and not the teacher's. The latter, however, sees what is needed and helps so that the children do make their own corrections. Let the following example of how one teacher handled such a situation speak for itself. Rules cannot be given.

Maria, quietly working with her balance, chose a pile of cotton wool and a small rubber. She placed them both on her balance and was surprised that the tiny rubber was heavier than the big fluff of cotton wool. She called her teacher to come and see. He showed interest and talked to her. Maria demonstrated how she came to her unexpected conclusion 'See? The rubber goes down and the cotton goes up.' Then the teacher asked her, 'Can you find something that is lighter than the cotton wool?' and went his way. Maria tried several objects until she found a peanut which was lighter than the cotton wool She took her book and wrote, 'I put cotton on one side and my rubber on the other. When I put a peanut, the cotton went down.' When her teacher saw this cryptogram he gave the following comments. To the first part he added, 'What did your balance look like?' and by the second part he asked, 'Where did you put the peanut?'

This teacher effectively helped Maria to make her notes better without creating fear or tension. It did not take Maria long to add her drawing of the balance with the cotton up and the side with the rubber down. She also wrote, 'The rubber was heavier. Then I put a peanut instead of the rubber, and the peanut was lighter'. And this she illustrated with a fresh drawing of the balance in reverse position. And, what is more, she thought it was all her own idea!

The tape recorder or 'audio' notebook

The use of a tape recorder should be mentioned here, acting as an 'audio notebook'. It can be introduced by the teacher as a way of helping children become aware of the value of making some kind of record of events as they happen. A group might switch on a tape recorder, say for 10 minutes, during an activity when they are watching something and talking to each other about what is happening. They should then listen to the recording to refresh their memories of all that happened. For some children who labour over writing, the frequent use of the tape recorder may be appropriate, while for others it should be used more selectively; the children should help decide when it is the best form of recording to use.

Occasional tape recording of group work has an additional benefit for the teacher who, through listening to a group discussion, can pick up clues to the children's ideas and reasoning expressed in his or her absence. If a recording is replayed with the teacher and group listening together there is the chance of challenging the ideas and of offering alternatives, as suggested in Chapter 7.

Notebooks, visual or aural, can become a source of inspiration to both the children and to their teacher, who is bound to notice the rich variety of the children's discoveries and interests and their charming ways of description and representation. All children who have learned to realize that their workbooks are their own means of expression increase their interest and ability in recording their work. It becomes, as it should, an integral part of their scientific activities.

Drawing, painting and modelling

It is very common for teachers to involve children in drawing, painting and modelling as part of science activity. It is uncommon, however, for teachers deliberately to set about improving the ability of children to draw, paint or model as part of their science programme. Perhaps the reluctance to evaluate the products that children create as part of science activity stems from a reaction against the excessively prescriptive and judgemental approach which was common some years ago.

'Mr Miller was very good at drawing. In fact, it was Mr Miller who first taught me that I couldn't draw. It was one day when he had drawn a big lemon on the board and told us to copy it. Anyone whose lemon was very good, said Mr Miller, would be allowed to draw its shadow. Shadows had to be done in black pastel and sometimes you couldn't help getting it all over your hands and your face. Once Ian Pratt did it on purpose and drew a beard and moustache on his face. I thought he looked quite nice, but Mr Miller didn't think so and said, "I'll give you beard and moustache, young man". We all watched very interestedly, but all he gave Ian was two straps on each hand. After that he collected all the black pastels from our boxes and only gave them out when it was time to do shadows.

On the day we were drawing lemons I was still filling in my lemon with yellow when Mr Miller came around to my desk and said, "And what, may I ask, is that supposed to be?" Before I could tell him it was going to be a lemon, he turned my book upside down and said, "No, I don't think it's meant to go that way either". Everybody laughed and then he said, "Oh well, I suppose we can't all be Michaelangelo" and wrote 4½/10 beside my lemon.'
Jean Holkner 'Their Monday Morning Blues'
The Age Newspaper, Melbourne (Australia)
2nd March 1982 (page 20)

Rejecting tight teacher control based on certainty of what is 'correct' leaves the problem of what teacher role to put in its place. Some guidelines for an interactive, but not intefering, teacher role come from thinking about the reasons for giving children opportunity to draw, paint and model in science. Among the various reasons that have been proposed the most common are that it will help children to observe, remember and communicate; also, as mentioned earlier in this chapter (page

99), the products can be used by teachers to understand the children's thinking better. Let us consider each of these in turn.

Representation as an aid to observation, recall and communication

Although there is no indisputable evidence to support the commonly held claim that making some representation of an object will improve observation, it does seem reasonable to suppose that if children are going to record their observations in some way they are likely to observe more closely. However to assume that this is always the case is to ignore the natural development in children's graphic skills. These skills develop through certain well-recognized stages. While there may be differences of opinion about the emphasis placed on certain characteristics of development, there is general agreement about the course it takes (such as scribble at 2–4 years, primitive schematic at 4–5 years, schematic at 6–9 years, mixed schematic at 10–12 years and true to appearance at 12+ years).

Most children in the primary school do not produce drawings which attempt truly to represent the objects in front of them. Instead their drawings are influenced by prior conceptions about the object. This is illustrated by some investigation in Australia of children's drawings of leaves. The children approached the task in the belief that it was important to record accurately the detail of the leaf edge but less important to record the venation accurately. Not surprisingly their drawings showed more attention to some features than to others. Younger children, when asked to draw several leaves, ceased to observe the actual leaves after a while and included a stem in their drawings of an elm leaf although no stem was actually visible on the leaf. These children were responding to the leaves in front of them as symbolic leaves. Stems and shapes are particularly prominent in young children's conceptions of leaves and so became the important part of what they 'saw'.

Thus if children are left to their own devices they become engrossed in their drawing or painting and stop observing the details of the objects they are representing. Consequently there will be no certain improvement in observation through the activity. The question then arises as to whether the teacher can or should do anything about this, and if so, what?

What the teacher can do is to help children shed their preconceptions and really see what is there. Drawing attention to particular features of an object is very important, features which relate to the purpose of the drawing or modelling. Children watching waterbirds feeding on a visit to a pond might be asked to look carefully at the beaks of the birds and then at the beaks of small birds feeding on the crumbs thrown on the grass round the pond. How would you describe the shape of a duck's bill, when it is open and when it is closed? How is it different from a pigeon's bill? Could a pigeon manage with a duck's bill and vice versa? When the children sit down, there and then on the grass, not later in the classroom, to draw the birds, the beaks might well be drawn more realistically than the rest of the duck. The drawings in Fig. 8.3 show the focusing effect of such discussion in the case of the drawing of a duck brought into the classroom.

Fig. 8.3

A great deal of what was said in Chapter 3 is relevant here, for the ways suggested for helping children to observe carefully serve equally to help them represent significant details relating to perception rather than preconception. It is worth reflecting on the word 'significant' in this context for a moment, reminding ourselves that it is important for the drawing or painting or modelling to have some purpose. To serve that purpose not all details will be relevant and therefore a photographic representation or accurate model is not necessarily the most useful. What we mean by 'accurate' is that which helps understanding of a particular point. If the ducks' beaks show that they help in water feeding then it may not matter that their tails are the wrong shape.

The second reason mentioned earlier for encouraging children to draw, paint or model was that it will help them remember what they have seen. Certainly research evidence supports the notion that children will remember their own reconstructions of objects and events. However, the value of this will obviously depend upon whether the representations are merely following preconceptions or whether they reflect an attempt to focus upon and understand some part of the object or event.

Similarly the third reason, (helping communication) sends us back to the same points about purpose and focus. Figure 8.4 shows the drawings produced by two children when asked, without teacher intervention, to draw a sheep's bone (a vertebra from its spine). The children have made different decisions about what should be communicated. The first child has produced a drawing which accurately reflects the shape of the bone from one perspective. However, the drawing does not show the cavity through which the spinal cord passes. The second child has decided that two drawings are needed, both showing the spinal cord cavity but one from the 'front' and one from the 'back'.

Neither of the children has given a clue as to the relationship between the size of the drawing and the size of the actual bone. This may or may not be important, depending on the purpose of the drawing. If the drawing is to show the general shape of vertebrae in one particular section of the spine of a sheep or to show the way in which the spinal cord is protected, there is no need to mention the actual size of the bone. However, in other circumstances, the size of the bone can be significant.

There is such a complexity of ideas and skills intervening between seeing something and producing some graphic or plastic representation of it. There is the perception, the taking in of the general scene, the recall of previous ideas, the challenging or otherwise of these ideas, the focusing, questioning, looking for clues to help understanding of what is there, selecting the medium to use for recording, the struggle to make the marks that fit the intention, the passing to and fro between the ideas, the object and the image. The teacher can help with all of these through discussion which links the purpose with the observation and with the medium through which it can be communicated. The latter, the medium, brings us to an area of overlap between science education and art education.

But children are not in the same position as that of the artist;

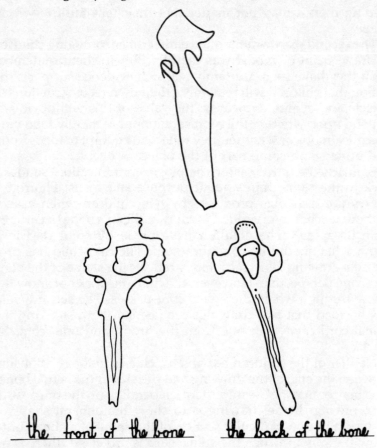

the front of the bone   the back of the bone

Fig. 8.4   *Childrens' drawings of bones*

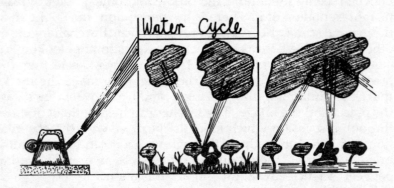

Fig. 8.5

they cannot know what brush, chalk, pencil, charcoal or waxed scraper board can do until they have experimented with them. Just as the teacher intervenes to stretch the vocabulary of children, so intervention is appropriate to extend the range of materials and instruments the children can use to develop their graphic skills. A pencil alone can produce a range of different marks. A teacher giving children small pieces of paper to cover in pencil marks of as many different kinds as they can is opening children to new ways of expressing their observations. This serves both to develop graphic skills and observational skills.

So, in summary, before embarking on a drawing or model discussion between teacher and children should help the children decide about:

1 The purpose, perhaps to excite, to inform, to show something that is beautiful or an interesting pattern.
2 The general form or details to focus upon.
3 The choice of materials suited to the amount of detail and the general impression to be conveyed.
4 How their existing ideas may influence what they produce. Bringing these out into the open may clear the way for seeing things which were there but not previously noticed (such as the pattern of veins and the texture of the surfaces of leaves as well as their size and shape).

Representation as a source of clues to children's thinking

A much-neglected use of the products of children's drawing, painting and modelling is as a guide to their thinking, that is, as a diagnostic tool. Fig. 8.5 illustrates this use. After demonstrating how water vapour coming from a bottle condenses on a cold plate, this child's teacher went on to explain the water cycle using the demonstration as an analogy. After the class discussion the children were asked to draw the water cycle. As can be seen from the presence of the kettle in the picture drawn by this child, she has not been able to grasp fully the link between the analogy used and the water cycle in nature.

Some researchers interested in investigating the concepts pupils have of various phenomena have found pupils' drawings to be a very powerful way of showing how pupils represent certain things to themselves. For example, to explore pupils' ideas about air, they showed the children a wide tube with a soap film formed across it, then warmed the bottom of the tube so that the soap film moved up as the air beneath it expanded

(Fig. 8.6)). The children were asked to draw the air and explain what made the soap film rise. (Novick and Nussbaum, 1981).

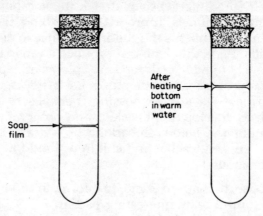

Fig. 8.6

The drawings were used to infer how the children thought air was constituted and what happened when it was heated. For example some seemed to consider air as made up of particles very close to each other, filling most of the space (Fig. 8.7a), for others the particles were smaller and moved upwards when they were heated (Fig. 8.7b) and others implied that the particles were moving and their movement was increased when they were heated (Fig. 8.7c).

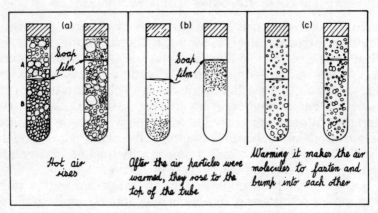

Fig. 8.7

The technique used here is a simple one, which teachers could adapt to enable children to convey how they see things and use themselves to try to understand the children's view. It is interesting to ask children to draw pictures to show how, for example, they think the dew forms on the grass overnight, what they think happens to food and drink that we swallow, what happens when you turn a water tap on, what keeps a floating boat up and a sunken wreck down in the water. Discussion with the child is important to interpreting their drawings, it must be remembered, otherwise the teacher could be falling into the same error as almost befell Louis' teacher (on pages 97 and 98).

The question underlying the teacher's role is whether children should be left to discover on their own the various connections between real objects and representations of them. Children's graphic skills develop through well-defined stages, but there is nonetheless a strong case for teacher intervention (though not of the kind used by Mr Miller!). The teacher's role is to help children extend and elaborate these skills, taking account of the stage they have reached, and so use them effectively in exploring and building their understanding of the world around.

Summary of main points

Communication can take various forms in science activities and can be regarded as part of the process of learning or as a product. All of the forms discussed here – discussion, making notes and using two- and three-dimensional forms of representation – have been considered as part of learning about things around and not simply as ways of making a neat written record, graph, diagram or model.

It has been a theme throughout this book that discussion should be included in all science activities. Discussion among a group of children alone helps them to try out ideas which are still in a somewhat unformed state and to hear a variety of ideas from others. The rather more formal discussion in small groups with a teacher present gives the teacher a chance to challenge children's ideas and offer some alternatives for them to consider. Whole-class discussion is the arena for sharing ideas which groups have already talked through and should be prepared to support with evidence. The result of explaining ideas and putting them together with others' gives each child a richer supply of ideas than he could obtain on his own. The discussion continues the learning process as well as creating a report on what has been found.

Children should become accustomed to using a notebook (sometimes aided by a tape recorder) for jotting down observations during activities. It has been suggested that these notes should be regarded as personal to the child, not ones to be 'marked' by the teacher. The role of the teacher is to help children find more efficient and effective ways of keeping notes and records, by introducing suggestions as and when these can be used. A delicate balance is required, for too much guidance too soon can lead to children recording what they think the teacher wants them to put down and the results they think they should get. But techniques and correct words can be offered without this over-direction and some suggestions have been given. The resulting notes and records are the children's own; valuable to them as *aides-mémoire* and valuable to the teacher as a source of information about children's thinking.

Non-verbal representation, in the form of drawings, models and paintings have their role in learning science. An important point, however, is that the purpose of producing the representation must be clear to the teacher and the children. Drawing will not necessarily improve observation unless it is preceded by some discussion of what might be relevant for the particular purpose of the drawing, and followed by a discussion in which certain features of the object are compared with the representation. Teachers should ensure that children are introduced to various techniques they might want to use in their representations and have some practice of relevant skills. Examples have been given of how children's preconceptions influence their drawing, paintings and models. It follows that studying these products can give a useful pointer to teachers as to how children believe things to be.

Guidelines for encouraging discussion

1 When children are working in groups, make it clear that you *expect* them to discuss with each other and to try to settle differences by finding evidence for one view or another.
2 Only start a discussion with children in small groups when they have something to tell you or to consult you about; if they are purposefully working on their own, leave them to it.
3 Find out the children's own ideas about a problem on which they want your help before offering your own; take part in discussing the problem as a member of the group as far as possible.
4 Give five or ten minutes' warning before a whole-class discussion so that groups can prepare themselves for reporting.
5 In a whole-class discussion make sure each group has its say on a topic before going on to another one.

6 Accept all points for consideration and let the children object to findings or ideas which don't fit in with their own; the disputed areas should be identified for further work.

Guidelines for helping children to keep records

1 Provide children with a notebook that they can use in their own way to keep some kind of record of their activities.
2 In group discussions ask children to use their notes to recall what they have done, so that they see the value of keeping a record.
3 Read through the notebooks occasionally, without correcting them but suggesting words or ways of organizing the information that will make the records more useful.

Guidelines for using drawing, painting and modelling

1 Discuss the purpose of making a drawing, and so on, with children before they embark on it, so that they focus on relevant features and ways of representing them.
2 Sometimes allow a free choice of materials and techniques for representation; at other times discuss the appropriateness of various possibilities beforehand.
3 Ensure children have at some time practised the techniques and know the range in the use of materials available to them.
4 Discuss the products but don't judge them, showing interest in discrepancies between the representation and the object and the children's reasons for them.
5 Study children's representations; notice what they treat in detail, what only cursorily, what they ignore, what they change. This will help in understanding what interests them and how they interpret what they see.

References

Barnes, D. *From Communication to Curriculum* (Harmondsworth: Penguin, 1976).

Bell, B. F. When is an animal not an animal? *Journal of Biological Education*, 1981, 15 (3), 213–18.

Bell, B. F. and Barker, M. Toward a scientific concept of animal, *Journal of Biological Education*, 1982, 16 (13), 197–200.

Cosgrove, M. and Osborne, R. J. *Electric Circuits* (Hamilton, NZ: Hamilton Teachers College, 1983).

Department of Education and Science *Children and their Primary Schools. Vol. 1* (London: HMSO, 1967).

Department of Education and Science *Primary Education in England* (London: HMSO, 1978).

Department of Education and Science. *Science at age 11, Report No. 1* (London: HMSO,1981).

Department of Education and Science, APU Science Report for Teachers: 1 *Science at age 11* (ASE Hatfield, 1983).

Freyberg, P. S., Osborne, R. J., and Tasker, C. R. The Learning in Science Project. In Harlen, W. (Ed.) *New Trends in Primary School Science Education* (Paris: UNESCO, 1983).

Galton, M. and Simon, B. *Progress and Performance in the Primary Classroom* (London: Routledge and Kegan Paul, 1980).

Harlen, W. *Guides to Assessment in Education: Science* (London: Macmillan Educational, 1983).

Harlen, W., Darwin, A. and Murphy, M. C. *Match and Mismatch: Raising Questions* (Edinburgh: Oliver and Boyd, 1977).

Learning through Science project (London: Macdonald, 1981–5).

Novick, W. and Nussbaum, J. Pupil's understanding of the particulate nature of matter: a cross-age study, *Science Education*, 65, 2, 1981, 187–96.

Nuffield Junior Science: Teacher's Guide: Apparatus (London: Collins, 1967).

Nussbaum, J. D. and Novick, S. Brainstorming the classroom to invent a model: a case study. *School Science Review*, 62 (221), 1981, 771–8.

Osborne, R. J. Towards modifying children's ideas about electric current, *Journal of Research in Science and Technological Education*, 1983.

Osborne, R. J. and Freyberg, P. *Learning in Science: the implications of 'Children's science'* (London: Heinemann Educational Books, 1985).

Science 5–13, Units for Teachers (London: Macdonald, 1972–5).

Symington, D. *Scientific Problems seen by Primary School Pupils*. Unpublished Ph.D. Thesis, Monash University, Australia, 1980.

Tasker, R. Two lessons in one, *SET*, 1, Item 8, (Wellington: NZCER, 1982).

Index